To the readers of this book,

Thanks for all your support
throughout my career!

Best Wishes

Tributes to Ty

I have always been favorably impressed with Ty Detmer. From the time I saw him enter his first game at BYU, I have known him to be a winner. More than this, however, he is a winner off, as well as on, the gridiron. Generous in his praise for the plays of his teammates, modest with regard to his own accomplishments, he has the respect of one and all who know him.

He is a person of principle and one who has the courage of his convictions. He and his lovely wife, Kim, form an unbeatable team.

I was proud of Ty's outstanding performance at the 1991 Holiday Bowl. As his collegiate football career concludes, I feel he will be equally successful in the professional ranks of football.

For Ty and Kim, there will indeed be life beyond football, for they have a love for their Heavenly Father and for all others.

—Thomas S. Monson
Second Counselor in the First Presidency
The Church of Jesus Christ of Latter-day Saints

Ty's the best-kept secret in America.

—Brent Musburger
CBS sportscaster, November 10, 1989

Ty Detmer is the best I have ever seen. . . . I have seen all the quarterbacks that you can possibly imagine playing football, and everything else, but I want to tell you something. I've watched this guy for three years, and I've watched him tonight. He throws the ball better than any guy I have ever seen. He is the best quarterback I have seen in college football. He threw a couple of passes tonight, amazing—and they are right on target.

—Coach Earle Bruce
Colorado State

I really like his coolness. If it was baseball and he was a pitcher, he'd be a pitcher who has every pitch. The fast ball is there. The curve ball is there. The slider is there. We had him stopped cold a few times, and he still was able to throw the ball across his body to complete a pass. He found guys who shouldn't have been open down the field.

—Coach Bobby Bowden
Florida State

He was sensational. The guy is like Houdini. He's better than we thought he was. He's a tremendous athlete.

—Coach Terry Donahue
UCLA

Detmer can move a team in the air with the best of them. He's poised, clever, and quick. He looks defensive backs off his target like a ten-year NFL veteran. Detmer has great touch. He knows where his receivers will be on the field. He delivers the ball to them as they break open. When his receivers are covered, he scrambles and picks up yards on his own. Sometimes he'll run, stop, and find an open man with an accurate pass. You can go on and on. The guy is an outstanding college quarterback.

—Mike Waldner
The *Daily Breeze*

I thought Ty was the best quarterback we've probably ever played against in all of my years at Penn State. He has a great feel for things. You rush five men and he knows you're in some kind of man-to-man. Then he'll come off the top and get it to his backs going one-on-one. You rush three, he can sense that you're rushing three. He just sits in there and waits till something develops down-field. If you go to an all-out blitz, he reads the blitz real well. . . . He's a superior competitor.

—Coach Joe Paterno
Penn State

As good a football player as Ty is, he is an even better person. It has never been "I" with him, but always "we." He always in-cluded his teammates and coaches in the accolades given him, and

has been an example to all of us of the competitive spirit, selfless-
ness, and keeping everything in perspective.

—Norm Chow
BYU quarterback and receiver coach

Ty is a fearless, confident, and composed competitor. The
players follow him and respect him, not only for his athletic ability, but even more for his character.

Ty has a field sense much like Jim McMahon. He knows everything that is happening on the field, offensively and defensively,
where everyone is on the field, and where they're supposed to be.

Ty told one of our receivers, who was supposed to run a route
over the middle, "If you're scared, don't play!" That's Ty Detmer.

—Lance Reynolds
BYU running back coach

Ty Detmer is the best college impact player I've ever seen. I've
played against three or four Heisman Trophy candidates, but if you
were starting a team, who would you want? Detmer. I think he
should win it. I think he deserves it. He does more for a football
team than anyone I've seen in a long time. He has great scrambling
ability, great sense of where the heat is. You know who he reminds
me of—and Detmer may have a better arm—is Fran Tarkenton.

—Coach Paul Roach
Wyoming

Even with all the success that has come to him, Ty is still very
coachable and down-to-earth. His competitive and winning attitude are an inspiration to everyone around him.

—Robbie Bosco
Quarterback coach and former BYU quarterback

Pound for pound, Ty may be the best who ever played the
game. When he hung it up Saturday, he hung up a Van Gogh, a
Rembrandt, a Picasso in a very fancy frame. Detmer's artistry will
stand as a standard in college football for years; maybe for all
time. BYU fans may not fully comprehend what they will miss—a
prototype quarterback, exemplary citizen. A bona fide hero.

The skinny Texan came from San Antonio as the most her-
alded football recruit ever collected by the Cougars. Five years

later, he fulfilled everything on the marquee, leaving nothing un-
done. On the field, Detmer will be remembered as a courageous
leader, fierce competitor, a playmaker with a very deep bag. Off
the field he is a very special man.

—**Dick Harmon**
Provo *Daily Herald* sports editor

The Florida State-Miami game was as scintillating a game, as
dramatic an afternoon as one could hope for. Yet, it wasn't the
most entertaining game of the day. Seriously.

That distinction belonged to San Diego State-Brigham Young,
at Jack Murphy Stadium, late. Very late. Ended-at-2:38-a.m.
(EST) late. For those of you who wimped out sometime before that,
what you missed was a 52-52 tie, in which each quarterback threw
for 500 yards, in which BYU trailed by 28 points in the second half
before Ty Detmer brought the Cougars back.

You might remember Detmer as last year's Heisman winner, a
wisp of a kid who everyone said was overrated. Sunday morning,
with a patch covering stitches over his left eye for a gash he suffered
in the first quarter, Detmer threw for 599. Bloody, cheek bruised,
Detmer was the damndest quarterback you've ever slept through.

—**Michael Wilson**
Washington Post, November 17, 1991

Probably few people in the history of this university have had
as much influence for good for this university as has this young
man who wore BYU football uniform number 14.

His influence for good here has reached far beyond what he
has done on the football field. Time after time I have been impressed by the remarkable insights that he has shown by his public comments. In every respect he has been a remarkable ambas-
sador for the university and for all the principles for which the university and Church stand.

—**Rex Lee**
President of Brigham Young University

Ty is the greatest football player to ever play the game. He's
the best, and when Koy is his age, I think he'll be every bit as
good as his older brother. I've set my personal goal, too; and when
I grow up, I want to be just like Ty.

—**Sonny Detmer**
Father and former coach

TY

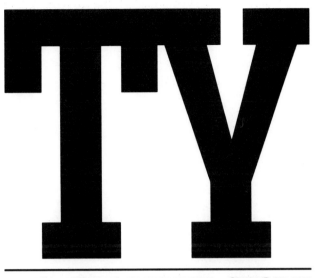

THE TY DETMER STORY

As Told To BRENTON YORGASON
With FRANK HERBERT & SONNY DETMER

Bookcraft
Salt Lake City, Utah

Frontispiece photograph © Doug Martin

Library of Congress Catalog Card Number: 92-71042
ISBN 0-88494-834-X

First Printing, 1992

Printed in the United States of America

Contents

*Go with the flow until you have
a chance to make something happen.
Work hard and play hard and often.*

—Ty Detmer

Preface

As I made the decision to tell my life story, I found myself experiencing many emotions.

First of all, I was concerned that by including many of my athletic statistics, from my earliest years in grade school to my concluding college game in the Japan Bowl, I might appear to be focusing on things that weren't very important. More than this, I wanted to share my own personal growth as an athlete. I also wanted to demonstrate to others—athletes and nonathletes alike—how much could be accomplished if they really believed in themselves. In addition, I knew that in sharing my stats I would be making a statement about my teammates and coaches, not just about myself. I also realize how temporary records and awards are, and that all records really are made to be broken—mine included.

I have always wanted to be a private person, so sharing my life's moments, both the ups and the downs, has been a different experience. I have made every effort to tell things as they actually happened, and not to blow the good or the bad out of proportion. If I have inadvertently stated anything inaccurately, I hope that any such oversights do not offend anyone. I have enjoyed a good twenty-four-plus years, and I hope that as you read my story you will feel the joy and the excitement that have followed me wherever I have gone. I don't believe that life should be too heavy, even though it involves a lot of hard work. To the contrary, I feel it should be fun and balanced, and that we should never take ourselves too seriously.

It is my hope that as you read the chapters that follow, you will enjoy the experiences I have chosen to share. I have many friends who have supported me throughout my life; and even though we may not have met, I want to thank you for your confidence in me as an athlete—but even more important, for your kindness to me as a friend.

I give special thanks here to the administration at Brigham Young University; as well as to the university's athletic department, particularly all those associated with the football program, including the coaching staff, trainers, team doctors, athletic directors, secretaries, and sports information people. Thanks also to those in the media who have greatly assisted in my career. While I am not able to name all of those coaches, athletes, friends, associates, and family who have influenced my playing career and my life, I here express my gratitude to all of them collectively; for without them this story could not be told.

In addition, Kim and I thank all the close friends and family who helped both with the wedding reception at the Triad Center in Salt Lake City and with the open house in Houston, Texas.

With regard to this book, I thank the many people who have made it possible. I thank both my mother, Betty, and Kim's mother, InaLee, as well as the three authors—my dad, Sonny Detmer; Kim's dad, Frank Herbert; and Brent Yorgason. I also thank both of my grandmothers for their support and assistance throughout my life.

Most of all, I thank Kim—not only for her help in the writing of this book, but especially for her example to me and her influence in my life. She is the greatest blessing to me, and I know that without her I would not be the person I am today.

Winning the Heisman

DECEMBER 1, 1990

My mind was several thousand miles to the east, in New York City, as Coach Norm Chow and I weaved in and out of the traffic of Honolulu, Hawaii, in our car. The temperature was nearly perfect, in the low eighties. I had just finished our pregame practice, and I was perspiring quite a bit. It wasn't so much that I had worked that hard in our pregame warm-up, because I hadn't. It was just that the three or four weeks building up to this day had been pretty hectic. In an hour or so I would be sitting at a press conference, with TV cameras everywhere. I just knew I would be glad that the suspense would be over, regardless of who won the Heisman Trophy. This was the fifty-sixth consecutive year that the award would be given—to the college football player who supposedly had contributed more to the game for that year than anyone else. Just the thought that I was even considered in this league was a sobering one.

I thought back then to that morning, when my roommate, Matt Bellini, had teased me about my chances of winning the Heisman. "You're not that good," he had kidded. "Besides, Raghib Ismail is from Notre Dame, and that makes him the shoo-in!"

I laughed, and felt happy that Matt had been my traveling roommate for the past two years. He was always joking around, and because he was such an outstanding athlete and football player, as well as a great friend, I respected him.

But still I felt anxious, as I knew that the teams from the Mountain West had a harder time even being recognized, let alone being seriously *considered* for such an honor. And I have to say that from where I stood it *was* a team award, even though it was given to the individual who supposedly contributed more to the game than any other player in a given season. I had told the guys all season long that if we won it, it would be because of what they contributed, and their performance on and off the field.

As Coach Chow and I worked our way through the traffic, just a block or so from Waikiki Beach, I noticed all of the beautiful palm trees swaying in the soft, tropical breeze. What a perfect setting, I thought, wishing my family could be there to enjoy it with me.

My thoughts then turned to the other great quarterbacks from the Y, and how they had really paved the way for this moment to be even possible for me.

The first real Heisman contender from BYU was Gary Sheide, who in 1974, when Archie Griffin won the award, finished eighth in the balloting. Gifford Nielsen finished sixth two years later, when Tony Dorsett won it. In 1979, Marc Wilson finished third, when Charles White won it. Then in 1980, when George Rogers won, Jim McMahon took fifth. The next year, when Marcus Allen won the Heisman, McMahon moved up to third. Two years after that, in 1983, Steve Young placed the highest that any BYU quarterback ever had: he took second place behind Mike Rozier. The very next year Robbie Bosco received enough votes to take third. That was the great year that Doug Flutie of Boston College won it. I remembered that one *very* well. Robbie placed third again the following year, which was when Bo Jackson won. Then in 1989, my sophomore year, I was lucky enough to place ninth. Andre Ware of Houston won that one, and I was really happy for him. He really had a great season!

"How's your younger brother, Koy, doing in the play-offs?" Coach Chow asked, breaking the silence and bringing my thoughts back to the present.

"Oh, he's doing all right. Actually, last week his team, the Mission High Eagles, won 24-14 over Alice High in the Texas play-offs. As a junior in just his sixth start of the season, he was twenty-one of thirty-two in passing for 333 yards. He'd thrown for 247 of those yards by halftime—can you believe that?"

"I'll bet he's having the time of his life," Coach Chow replied.

"Yessir, he is! Even though he's only started for half the season, he leads the state of Texas in passing yards and has thrown thirty-five TD passes. I'm really happy for him, and I know he'll have a great senior year, too! I know my dad, Sonny, is sure looking forward to it."

"Ty," Coach continued, changing the subject a bit, "how many TD's did you get during your best high school season?"

I've always felt a little awkward quoting stats about myself, but I answered, "Oh, about thirty-five or thirty-six . . ."

I appreciated the coach giving me a ride back from practice in a car; that way I didn't have to wait around for the bus. It felt good to get out of the stadium a little quicker.

My thoughts turned again to the Heisman, and to an interview I had had the Monday before with a network of sportswriters on what they call a tele-conference call.

"I've downplayed it long enough," I had told them.

"I am really looking forward to Saturday and the announcement on the Heisman. It will make a long, long week this week, but I'm excited.

"My approach to all this," I had continued, "is to expect the downside of not getting the award. Then if it comes it will be a big surprise. I am tired of the questions about it and of forcing myself to downplay the Heisman. This is it."

And I *was* tired of it, too. It seemed that it was almost the only thing anyone around me wanted to talk about, and they always asked me the same question—whether I thought I had a shot at it.

Coach Edwards was also on the tele-conference interview, and I was taken aback by what he had said. In speaking of me he said, "Inside that little frame burns a furnace. Ty has shattered the NCAA record book; he has been consistent week in and week out in a roller-coaster season when he's been in and out as the front-runner. And he has handled the pressure as well as anyone. His passing efficiency is on target to be the best of all time."

The sportswriters had asked Coach Edwards if he would feel a little vindication on the part of BYU's past quarterbacks, who did not win the Heisman, if I finally did. I agreed with what Coach told them: "I think every one of our quarterbacks of the past would feel they owned a part of the trophy."

I reflected, then, on our trip over to play Hawaii, and how I had felt bad, thinking that we wouldn't win the Heisman. But when we arrived and I read *USA Today*'s articles, I felt pretty happy. Many prominent people had been asked to comment about me and whether they thought I should win the Heisman. I had saved the newspaper, and it made me feel good to think that I had so many friends who supported me.

Larry Guest, of the *Orlando Sentinel*, was the first one quoted, and he said, "I think Detmer has proved himself in a spectacular fashion over the years. I don't regard BYU's opposition in the Pop Warner category as some national media do. He had a pretty good day against Miami, and they have a fair-to-middling team."

Andy Gardiner, of the *Burlington (Vermont) Free Press,* said: "What stood out for me on Detmer is that although he padded his statistics against sub-par competition, his performance against Miami convinced me he could get the job done."

David Pickle, of the *Houston Chronicle,* was quoted as saying: "I was going to vote for Shawn Moore, but he broke his thumb. Detmer had his second sensational year in a row. When it was all considered, he was the most consistent. I'm glad I waited."

Earl Campbell, the 1977 winner of the Heisman, was especially nice. He said: "I think the Rocket is a very good football player, but I had to vote for Detmer because I think he has done more for his team. I just like him as a candidate."

Craig Sager, of the Turner Broadcasting Systems, said: "If you watch an entire Notre Dame football game, there will be four or five plays where the Rocket makes a big impact; and that's what you see on the highlight shows on TV. If you watch BYU, you see that on every play Ty is a factor."

Keith Dunnavant's comments were also kind. He writes for the *National,* and he said: "Ty is such a phenomenal athlete, he's there on every play."

One of the quarterbacks I had always admired was Doug Flutie, who, as I mentioned, had won the award in 1984. In making a flattering comparison of the two of us, Scooter Hobbs, of the *Lake Charles (Louisiana) American Press,* said: "Normally I'm skeptical of BYU numbers. But when I saw Detmer play, I got the feeling he had that Doug Flutie on-field charisma. I liked his on-field presence."

Well, these folks had seen it as a two-man race, and I guess by now it was. In the sports section of *USA Today* they devoted two entire pages to the Heisman race, and the articles were very favorable of our winning it. It really made me feel great when the lead article was titled "Heisman Race Is Close to a Ty—Detmer Edges Out Ismail in Survey." When I read that, I felt pretty good, and I actually thought we had a chance to win.

THE ANNOUNCEMENT

When we arrived at the Princess Kaiulani Hotel, where we were staying, I first went to my room. I then went down to the pool, where the press was setting up their lights and cameras for the Heisman announcement from New York.

I sat down on the chair they had put there for me, and those in charge hooked me up to a headphone that allowed me to listen to the Heisman candidate interviews that were being held in New York. I could also see what was happening on the same TV program, and I enjoyed what the other Heisman finalists had to say. They were great players, and again I felt honored to even be in their company.

The longer I sat there, the more I realized that this was the longest hour of my life! It seemed that they'd never get the announcement made. So I just sat there and waited. I thought of my family and how they felt a part of it all, and maybe that's why I was so happy. More for them than for me. My dad is an old softie, and I knew he'd be emotional, especially if we won.

I also thought of someone else, and that was a girl back at the Y. She was my best friend actually, Kim Herbert. Kim and her family had really supported me during my college years, and I felt pretty good about how things were going between us. Her last words to me before I left Salt Lake City were, "Ty, I have no idea if you'll win the Heisman or not. But I do know that you deserve to win, because you have done the most."

Of course Kim was always talking about me that way, and even though I was continually surprised by her confidence in me, I still felt pretty good that she would support me the way she did.

Even though I had been slow to do it, before leaving Utah I had asked Kim to go with me to New York, in case we won. I hadn't wanted to get her hopes up, but still I wanted her to plan for the trip if the votes came out in our favor.

By this time people were standing around the announcement area, wishing me good luck; but I was pretty uncomfortable. The lights were hot, and I was perspiring as I watched the TV and listened to the buildup. Pretty soon the team arrived, and I invited anybody who wanted to join us to come down and be part of the announcement. We were all pretty excited by this time, and Coach Edwards and Coach Tuckett (who was actually the athletic director) were even there, along with Rex Lee, the president of BYU.

Finally, the last commercial ended, and the announcement was about to be made. I was the only one who could hear, because I was wearing the headphone, and so I just sort of tuned everyone else out and listened.

The man making the announcement said, "The winner of the 1990 Heisman Trophy is . . . Ty Detmer, *Ty Detmer of BYU* . . . Ty Detmer!"

When the announcer first said my name, my heart jumped, and I broke into a wide smile. I made a shaking motion with my right fist and said, "All right! We got it!" Coach Tuckett was to my right, Coach Edwards was sitting to my left, and some of the players were sitting around us. I turned to Coach and he broke into a big cheese grin, as wide as I'd ever seen. He threw his arms into the air and then gave me a big bear hug. I think he was every bit as happy as I was, because our team had finally won it! It had been a long time coming. To tell the truth, when they began the announcement I started to tingle. When they said my name I was stunned, then a little shocked. I couldn't speak, really, so Coach Edwards and I just hugged each other.

I didn't know it at the time, but the TV program then switched to a shot of my folks, who were in Kingsville, Texas, getting ready to coach a high school play-off game there at a neutral site. When they said my name, my dad just broke down and cried on Mom's shoulder. Mom was pretty strong, though, even though she was pretty emotional, too. They were pretty happy for us.

The TV show then ran some action shots of our team scoring touchdowns. While I was throwing touchdown passes, Carly Simon was singing, "Nobody does it better. Makes me feel sad for the rest. Nobody does it half as good as you. Baby, you're the best." Next the Beach Boys sang, "Round, round, get around, I get around." And then while they were showing me getting killed by some of the great defenses we'd played, Pat Benatar sang, "Hit me with your best shot!" I don't know that I ever wanted to get hit with *any* shot, but the TV program producers had fun with it, so I guess it wasn't so bad. The worst hit they showed was of me doing a 360-degree somersault after getting hit at San Diego State's end zone. Of all the highlights they showed, though, my favorite one was of me breaking away from the Miami defense before throwing a touchdown pass that ended up winning the game for us.

At one point during this two-minute run of film clips they even showed me as a little YMCA flag football player running for a touchdown. I guess my folks had given them that. I still remember how good it felt to make that touchdown. The clips ended with all the Cougar fans running onto the field after we beat Miami, and in the middle of the screen was a *Sports Illustrated* cover (which of course hadn't come out yet) that read, "Ty's Prize."

Actually, I never did think of it as *my* prize. It was an

award that took many years to win, with lots of great quarterbacks and football players contributing. And it was an award that all of my teammates worked the entire season to win. You don't win an award like that without great players like Andy Boyce, Chris Smith, Matt Bellini, all the offensive line, and then all the other great players on our team. It was an honor to represent them.

Coach Edwards and I had to stay behind and have an interview with the New York press corp. Finally, after what seemed like forever, the questions began.

"How do you feel right now?" one reporter asked.

"It's great, especially for Coach Edwards. He's had a lot happen to him over the years, but never the Heisman. It's a great day for him. He's waited a long time, and I'm happy for him. He deserves it."

"Do you have any others that you're happy for?" another reporter asked.

"Yessir, I do. I'm happy that my grandfather Hubert Detmer is alive to see the honor. He's been hanging on, and if this went on for another year he might not be here to share it."

They also interviewed Matt Bellini, who had teased me so much before the announcement. I really appreciated what he said: "It makes you proud to know you had something to do with it. To be a member of this team and play with Ty has been a great experience that I'll never forget. I'm as proud as I could be."

The press conference lasted about twenty minutes, and I was glad when it was over.

We were about to leave when Mark Smith, Rich Kafusi, and Alema Fatisemanu all decided to have some fun. They grabbed me and threw me into the pool. I guess I deserved it, because they sure had fun doing it.

Walking back to the room, soaking wet, I really tried to put it all out of my mind so I would be ready to play Hawaii.

I had a few minutes, so I called my dad's parents,

"Maw Maw" and "Paw Paw," to share the news of the award with them. They were pretty excited and proud that we had won, and Maw Maw said, "We always knew you would get it!"

I then called Kim to let her know that because we'd won, she now had to pack her bags for New York. But when the phone rang in her room, all I got was her answering machine. I was pretty disappointed, so I just left a message for her.

THE GAME WITH HAWAII

"How are ya feeling?" Matt asked after I had hung up the phone from trying to call Kim.

"Well, other than feeling bad that I didn't find Kim home, I'm doing all right. Actually, I'm more relaxed than I've been in several weeks . . . so I don't know if that's good or bad."

"We'll soon see," Matt added encouragingly. His mother had flown over for the game, and so he wanted to play well for her. But I think the whole team was having a big emotional letdown—a big relief, actually. It was going to be hard to get up for the game, but soon we were on our way to the stadium to get taped and ready to play.

Sometime later, after we had warmed up and had received our last-minute instructions from the coaches, we were back on the field ready to play. Following the coin toss, the officials held up the kickoff so they could honor us for the Heisman. It was really a nice gesture.

The game soon started, and I'll have to say that it was good to finally get moving around and doing something. But neither team was ready to play, really. They came out flat because they had beaten us so badly last year; and we came out flat because of all the emotions of winning the Heisman. Hawaii was fortunate to score first, though, and they never looked back from there.

Most of the folks back home figured that Hawaii had a personal vendetta to make me look bad, but it wasn't that way at all. Most of the players were congratulating me and feeling that it was a pretty big day for the WAC, not just for us. So they weren't out to get me, or anything like that.

Well, they had beaten us 56-14 last year, and that had hurt. But it hurt even worse for them to take it to us two years in a row. The game finally ended, with the score being 59-28. This knocked us all the way from number four in the national polls to number thirteen. After the game I just wanted to shower and get out of the stadium. But I stayed for another press conference, and someone asked me if I would rather have won the game than the Heisman Trophy. "I'd trade the trophy," I answered honestly. Then I continued: "That's a tough question, because it's such a big honor. But if we would have won, we'd be sitting here with a chance for the national championship, and there's no bigger honor than that in college football."

RETURNING HOME TO PROVO

The interviews finally ended, and before long we were in an airplane taxiing down the runway for our flight home. I was physically and emotionally drained because of the game, but I also knew that this was one of the happiest days of my life, and as Coach Edwards had said, there're always things worse than losing a ball game.

About six hours later, when we finally arrived in Salt Lake City, I was not thinking so much about the game as I was the many Cougar fans who met us at the airport. Kim was there too, and that made me happy. She smiled and said, "I'm sorry I missed your call, Ty. I feel really bad."

"That's okay," I said, returning her smile.

"Actually, I thought you would be busy with interviews and getting ready for the game, so I went out to dinner. I had to celebrate with my roommates, even if you weren't here."

Later that night, as I was sitting alone in my room in Provo, it all began to set in. I knew then that I had been lucky enough to be part of something really special. What I didn't realize was that as a result of the Heisman my life would never be the same. It was as if all of a sudden I didn't belong to just *me* or to my family; I belonged to everyone else—the school, the community of Provo, the state of Utah, and even the country as a whole.

Monday morning came, and before I knew it I had spoken to a rally in a parking lot, had received the key to the city from Mayor Joseph Jenkins, and had been honored to have "Ty Detmer Day" declared. Gary Binford of the *Daily Sports News* quoted me as saying, "I've been a little bit busier than I thought. I didn't think it could get much worse, but it's big-time here now."

One of the things that really surprised me was how much the reporters talked about my supposedly deciding to pass up my senior year at the Y by turning pro. I laid all that to rest, telling them I would honor my commitment to Coach Edwards and the school by returning for my last year of eligibility. In the final part of Binford's interview I pretty much said how I felt: "We've got a brand new team coming up next year . . . a lot of young guys. I'm not looking for next year to be better than this year, though. I'll try to be a team leader . . . just go out and lead, and have a good time."

Monday was also a day of going to class and getting ready for our trip to New York. My folks had made arrangements to come, along with my two sisters, and Kim and I were supposed to meet them at the hotel in downtown Manhattan.

I had known Kim Herbert for three years, and by this time we were pretty much going steady. We had been going together now for two months, and we were both looking forward to spending time together in New York so that we could really see where things were with each other.

On Tuesday morning, before flying to New York, Coach Edwards and I had to speak at a luncheon of the Salt Lake Chapter of the Cougar Club. Kim had to buy some clothes and get her hair done, so I went up to Salt Lake with Coach. The luncheon was at the Lion House, and our Salt Lake City fans were really kind to us.

After we were through speaking, Coach took me over to Kim's folks' house, where I waited for her to arrive.

Kim was late getting her hair done, and when I arrived at her folks' home after the luncheon I telephoned her Provo apartment to see if she was there. That's where she was, still packing, but she left right then, picked me up about a half hour later, and we headed for the airport.

When we finally arrived at the terminal, I told her not to say anything to the reporter, because all he would care about was getting his story. But when we saw him, Kim ran up to him and confessed, "It's my fault that we're late! I was late picking up Ty."

The reporter was a gentleman and laughed along with us. He then wrote a really nice article about the Y, and because the plane was late in boarding we made it in the nick of time.

TO NEW YORK CITY AND THE HEISMAN

When we arrived in New York, Kim and I were both excited to see such a big city, even though it was nearly midnight. Even so, I knew things were going first-class when Heisman representatives were there to give us the red-carpet treatment. We were picked up by a limo, and that was the first time we had ridden together in a limousine. The big city didn't disappoint us, either. It was really kind of overwhelming, with all of the tall skyscrapers and the cars and trucks going everywhere, even at that time of night.

On our way into the city, we had what, for us, was a scary moment. When we were stopped at a traffic light, an old man who looked like he lived on the streets came up to the window. Our driver, who had been a police officer, rolled the window down just an inch to see what the man wanted. The man said that he needed $36.00 for a part on his car, but that he had only $34.50. So he wanted the difference of $1.50. Kim and I looked at each other, and we just knew we were about to get mugged and that we wouldn't be alive to get the Heisman after all! But just then a police officer drove up and took care of the man, who had obviously been drinking, and we proceeded to our hotel.

We stayed at the Downtown Athletic Club Hotel, and because Kim and I had arrived a day before my family's arrival, the two of us went into a lounge, where we met the president of the Club, as well as the famous Doak Walker. But we were pretty tired by this time, and so even though we were excited about being in New York, we checked into our rooms, and I was asleep within minutes.

Wednesday morning was spent signing footballs and posters for the Club and meeting with the Heisman officials. (I'm kind of clumsy, by the way, so when I was signing posters I accidentally swiped at my light blue pants with the black magic marker I was using, and the marker made quite a line down one leg of my pants. It was by the crease, though, so I hoped no one would notice.) On this occasion the Heisman officials gave us some sweaters and other memorabilia, including four Heisman watches. I was excited about the watches because I could give one to my ailing grandfather, Paw Paw, as well as to my dad and to Kim's dad.

THE HISTORY OF THE HEISMAN MEMORIAL TROPHY

One of the other gifts we received was an extensive Heisman program booklet. Kim and I enjoyed learning from the booklet the history of the famous Heisman award:

As the Heisman Memorial Trophy takes on added stature and significance with every passing year, the man for whom the award is named fades ever deeper into the background. Few have even the vaguest notion of who Heisman was.

John W. Heisman was only a little fellow, physically. Yet he was one of the giants of the gridiron, an inventive football genius whose impact on football has been enormous.

Probably no man knew more about the history of football or knew more of the immortals of the game than John W. Heisman.

A nagging voice of conscience, he bedevilled the Football Rules Committee into legalizing the forward pass. Historians credit him with instituting the center snap a year before Amos Alonzo Stagg did. He introduced his Heisman Shift, one of the most feared offensive formations of his day, at Georgia Tech, and produced three unbeaten teams with it.

For thirty-six years, Heisman was a top-ranking coach at Auburn, Clemson, Georgia Tech, Penn, Washington and Jefferson, and Rice, among other colleges. He ranked in the upper echelon with Stagg, Dr. Harry Williams, Pop Warner, Percy Haughton, Bob Zuppke, Hurry-Up Yost, Knute Rockne and the other titans who operated during the period from before the turn of the century through the Golden Twenties. In his time, Heisman, Stagg and Warner constituted the "Football Trinity."

As football became rougher and tougher with flying wedges and mass plays, Heisman became worried. His imaginative mind saw the forward pass as the salvation of the sport. He hounded Walter Camp, the Rules Chairman, for three years, but couldn't budge him. He then bypassed Camp and enlisted John Bell and Paul Dashiell of the Committee. In 1906, the pass was legalized.

The most historic game of the Heisman career came when his Georgia Tech team swept over Cumberland by a score that probably will never be matched as a record high. The score was 222 to 0.

After playing football at both Brown and Penn, Heisman began his coaching career at Oberlin College in 1892. His first team had a perfect record. Thirty-six years later he retired. At that time, he became the Athletic Director of New York's Downtown Athletic Club, the organization that perpetuates his memory with the Heisman Memorial Trophy.

The Heisman Memorial Trophy Award is presented each year to the Outstanding College Football Player of the United States by this organization.

We were impressed by what we learned about Mr. Heisman and how much impact he had on the game. We also thought it was interesting that the forward pass, which Heisman introduced into the game of football, is the part of the game that has allowed me to accomplish what I have with the teams I have played on.

MY ONE REAL IDOL

As I thought of Mr. Heisman and his level of achievement, I thought of the one football player whom I would classify as my idol as I was growing up. His name is Roger Staubach, who played for Navy. After winning the Heisman in 1963, Roger had a fantastic career for the Dallas Cowboys and was later inducted into the NFL Hall of Fame. Those accomplishments were great, but the thing that set him apart from the others was his decency as a human being, and his desire to be a true Christian. He was my role model, not just in the way he could quarterback a team to the Super Bowl, but also when he was out of the limelight and was quietly helping people. And, too, he was from Texas, and I wanted to be someone else from that great state who could be called a winner in life as well as in football, just as he was. I think that everyone should have an idol to look up to, and for me it was Roger.

"You're daydreaming, Ty," Kim said, bringing me back to reality. "We've got to take these things back to your room, and then we can see New York."

Needless to say, I had learned not to argue, especially with a woman, and so we did just as she said.

After we took our memorabilia to my room, we were escorted around New York by a very nice hostess whose name was Bernadette. We also had to tape a Coca-Cola advertisement for the High School Athletic Association.

The rest of the day was given to us to enjoy however we wanted. So we took off and had a great time sightseeing. We went to the Hard Rock Cafe, and then the hostess took us to the famous F.A.O. Swartz Toy Store, where we walked around and played many of the video games they had set up there for demonstration.

After that, we returned to the hotel. My mom and two sisters had arrived by this time, and we were able to see them and share our excitement with them. We knew there would be a full evening of activities, so we all rested for a few minutes and then got ready for the first formal reception.

THE FORMAL FESTIVITIES

At five-thirty that evening I picked Kim up at her room, and we went to the cocktail reception, which was held in the Gotham Room. It was something, too—probably more fancy than anything I had ever seen. We visited with as many people as we could, and met a lot of the former Heisman winners and the directors of the Downtown Athletic Club.

A little before seven o'clock we went to the Heisman Room, where we enjoyed a very nice dinner/dance. The music was by Tommy Furtado and his orchestra, and even though I was really nervous, it was pretty romantic. I could tell Kim was having a good time, because we laughed a lot and just kind of felt that we belonged together.

Kim and I sat at the table and received our menu for the meal—and neither of us could even pronounce most of the things on the menu, let alone know what the words meant.

Those attending this first evening of festivities included the officers and governors of the Downtown Athletic Club, members of the Heisman Memorial Trophy Committee, and former Club presidents. The previous fifty-five Heisman winners, with their partners, were also in attendance, so it was pretty impressive company.

During the dance, Jim Plunkett's wife and someone else's wife introduced themselves to us, and even though we had not met Jim, his wife asked me to dance with her. I was pretty nervous about this because I don't really like to dance. But I was a good sport and went out and danced with Mrs. Plunkett. What made dancing especially difficult was that at first we were the only two on the dance floor. But soon a few more couples joined us, so I didn't feel so conspicuous.

We finally left, I dropped Kim off at her room, and were we ever exhausted! It had been quite a day, but being in New York with Kim was well worth it!

The next morning, which was Thursday, I attended the High School Football Stars Breakfast. This was at eight o'clock in the Heisman Room, and even though the partners were invited, they didn't really have to attend. So while Kim came later for breakfast, I went early and was able to speak to them and share my philosophy of being successful in life.

I was impressed that the Downtown Athletic Club was so prestigious and yet was organized to encourage young athletes to excel. They really made a fuss over these kids, and it was fun to be there to say something that, I hoped, would help them reach for their potential. Then we ate breakfast and signed posters, and they took lots of pictures. I especially enjoyed rubbing shoulders with the former Heisman winners who were present; it was great to see that they were just normal people. At that time we met Jim Plunkett, whose wife had asked me to dance the night before.

These guests had always been men and athletes that I had looked up to and admired, and now to be with them and to have them be so friendly was really great. Up until then I was happy we had won and that the trophy would be given to BYU; but what I didn't realize until that moment was that my winning had also admitted me to a close-knit fraternity of Heisman winners. It was really something!

When this was over, I went up to a room in the New York Marriott Marquis Hotel, where they were holding a press conference, and relaxed. As I mentioned, my mother, Betty, had arrived the day before with my sisters, Dee, age twenty-one, and Lori, age ten. It was great being with them all, and they were excited to be in New York City, just as we were. So Kim and my mom and sisters went out to the Statue of Liberty and toured that, while I had a much-needed nap.

After a while, I had to leave in order to attend the press conference. The national media had to be included, and they were good people.

THE FORMAL AWARDS CEREMONY

My family was ready for the evening awards ceremony by then, and of course I was wearing a tux. I sort of felt like a penguin, being dressed like that, but I felt kind of good, too, knowing that the whole event was to honor BYU. The rest of our party was asked to dress up, as well. For the men it was a black-tie affair, and for the ladies it was cocktail dresses. Everyone looked like they were ready for a night on the town.

My family and other guests were then taken by bus to the Marriott Hotel. I was already there, attending the press conference.

When the others arrived, we joined back up and were all escorted into a VIP reception in the Westside Ballroom. We met even more folks there, and it was enjoyable being there with Coach Edwards and the rest of the guests from Provo.

This was also the first time I had seen my dad during the trip. It sure was nice seeing him.

"Ty," he said, as we embraced, "this is the big time, and I'm proud of you."

"Yessir, I know," I answered, smiling.

Well, he was always emotional, as I've said, and he just kind of watered up in his eyes and hugged me again. We then met quite a few other athletes, including Harold Carmichael, who had been a receiver for the Philadelphia Eagles while I was growing up. He hadn't won the Heisman, but he was invited as a special guest. He was really nice to my family. Jim Taylor was also there, and we got to speak with him. Actually, my dad had ridden over to the Marriott with Jim on the shuttle, and so he had already met him. We also enjoyed meeting Earl Campbell. I had always liked seeing him play at Texas when I was growing up, and because I had met him once before I really enjoyed introducing him to Kim and my family. Kim especially liked Earl.

From this reception we were taken to the Broadway Ballroom for the dinner and awards ceremony. I felt anxious and excited all at the same time, because I knew this was what it was all about.

We had been given Heisman badges to wear, with Brigham Young University ribbon streamers attached, so we all looked pretty official.

Mr. Denis M. Leahy, who was chairman of the Heisman Memorial Trophy Committee, made the presentation, and I was really happy for President Lee, Coach Edwards, athletic director Glen Tuckett, and the other guests from the Y. They really deserved to be there.

During the ceremonies, Earl Campbell made a speech, and he said, "I would like to welcome Ty's family and his *friend*, Kim. I know they don't have girlfriends out there in Utah." Everyone laughed, and I was kind of embarrassed but proud all at the same time.

When Mr. Leahy handed me the trophy, it was kind of heavy and awkward, so it fell against my chest, and everybody thought I was going to drop it. But I wasn't. I was just trying to get a better grip on it. After all, by then I was bench pressing about "a-buck-oh-five" (105 pounds). Just kidding!

Following the ceremony, we were all shuttled back over to the Downtown Athletic Club, where we were staying. They had another reception there, and Dad fit right in, telling one football story after another. He can talk for hours about football, and he sure seemed to be enjoying himself.

THE GREATEST MOMENT OF ALL

Finally, about three in the morning, we were pretty tired, so I asked Kim if she wanted me to take her up to her room.

"My pumps are killing me," she said, and so I took

her up to change. While she was changing, I went up to my room to change, and then I went back down and took her back to the reception.

After that, we went up to my room for a while. The room was a true suite, and had a lounge area with sofas and a TV and telephone. I was expecting a call from a radio talk show, and so I thought it wouldn't be too inappropriate if Kim waited in the sitting lounge with me. We really hadn't been alone together much during the entire two days we had been in New York, and I had some things I wanted to say to her.

We were sitting there, visiting, when I knew it was now or never for me to tell Kim how I felt about her. I felt kind of awkward about it, but I took a deep breath, turned to her, and said, "Well, Kim, I just wanted to tell you how much I love you, and I'm really glad that you came on the trip with me." I didn't know how to say it, really, so I just kind of threw the words into the sentence.

There was dead silence for what seemed like forever, and I was really worried that I had blown it. But she finally broke the silence and said, "Ty, I don't know if you were trying to say that you love me . . . but . . . I love you, too."

"Oh, man . . . ," I sighed, "I was worried that I'd ruined it! Kim, you really didn't have to say it just because I said it."

"No, Ty, I really meant what I said. I really do love you."

I was relieved to hear her response, so then we kissed, with my heart beating a hundred miles an hour. It was the perfect ending to a perfect day.

MEETING BOB HOPE AND OTHERS

The next morning we all had to leave on separate flights because I had to go to Ft. Lauderdale, Florida, and tape the Bob Hope Christmas Special with the Associated Press All-America team. So I told everyone good-bye and handed the Heisman Trophy to Dad.

"You know, Paw Paw has most of my other trophies, Sonny, and I know how much this will mean to him. So please give this to him and to Maw Maw."

Dad knew how much his father meant to me, and how many hours he had worked and played with me during my younger years; and so he was really pleased to take the trophy back to Paw Paw's in San Antonio. I just wish I could have been there to give it to him myself.

I found out later that after we left, Kim fell asleep, and she barely awakened in time to catch her flight back to Salt Lake City. I felt bad, too. She was really sick the whole flight home—so, for her, it was not a good way to end a vacation.

But I caught my flight to Miami, and then just relaxed that day at the Embassy Suites Hotel, waiting for the taping at a local high school. I was the first of the players to arrive, and I was looking forward to seeing Chris Smith, who had also been named on the team.

He finally arrived, and while the other players went out and partied, Chris and I went down to a Subway sandwich shop, got a couple of sandwiches, and then went back to our room and ate, and watched TV.

Friday morning came too quickly, but we were excited to meet Mr. Hope and to be with him. He surely didn't look to be eighty-six years old, either, even though his makeup did help with how good he looked on TV. But Mr. Hope joked with us during the filming, and we had a really nice time.

That evening I flew to Cincinnati, where I stayed for two days, attending the Chevrolet College Football Awards program. I was fortunate to be named the Chevrolet Offensive Player of the Year there at the College Football Hall of Fame Center. It was really humbling to receive that award, especially with all of the memorabilia at the Hall of Fame. Chris Zorich, of Notre Dame,

was there with me, and he was named the Defensive
Player of the Year. He is really a great guy, and I gained
a lot of respect for him.

After the ceremonies, I went and visited relatives, including Edwin and Londalea Swinford, in Rising Sun, Indiana. Londalea is Paw Paw Detmer's sister, and we've always been close to her family. But I hadn't seen them for
some time, so it was great to just relax at their home and
get caught up on what was happening with their family.

HOME, AT LAST

I then flew home to Utah, and Kim and her family all
met me at the airport. When I walked off the plane, I
handed Kim some airsickness bags and said, "Here,
these are for you. One of the flight attendants recognized
me, and she said that you needed these during your
flight and that you left them." Well, she was embarrassed, but we all had a good laugh.

Kim had already given her dad the Heisman watch
and hat and had given her family the other mementos, so
they were pretty happy for us. I also found out at this
time that Kim's parents felt that something was happening between Kim and me, I guess because you don't just
go around giving Heisman watches away. But I was feeling pretty good about us, and I wanted them to know
how much I appreciated them and their support. They
had become great friends to me over the past three years,
and even though Kim and I had only dated for a couple
of months, they could see that things were getting pretty
serious.

Little did I realize, as Kim and I drove back to Provo,
how permanently our lives would change—because of the
Heisman experience, and because of the brief, awkward
moment in New York when we acknowledged for the
very first time that we were rapidly falling in love.

Roots and Beginnings

ANCESTORS

I feel very indebted to think of the many *great* great-grandparents I have had, both on the Detmer and the Spellman side. They gave up their homes in Europe to settle in the United States, and here they provided a life that would eventually give me so much opportunity. They were men and women who believed in God, who fought bravely for the independence of our country as well as for the great state of Texas, and, more important, who believed in being good people.

My dad descended from courageous, God-fearing fighting men. Among other immigrants from Germany, two of them were decorated heroes of the American revolutionary war.

On my mom's side, several progenitors distinguished themselves, beginning in Plymouth, Massachusetts, in the 1600's. One of them was the first governor of Massachusetts Bay Colony, another the first minister of Bridgewater, Massachusetts. It was said that this minister was a "gracious, faithful, humble servant of God." Mom's ancestors were among the first three hundred to join the famous Stephen F. Austin's colony in settling Texas. Many of these ancestors are buried in the private Spellman Family Cemetery in Nopal, Texas.

MY PARENTS—SONNY AND BETTY SPELLMAN DETMER

My mother, Betty Lou Spellman, was born in El Campo, Texas, in 1944. The third of six children, she spent her childhood in El Campo. Dad was born the same year in Beaumont, Texas, and was raised in Lawrenceburg, Indiana.

At age sixteen, after receiving a baseball and basketball scholarship to play for Wharton Junior College in Wharton, Texas, Dad left his home in Indiana and drove south for keeps. He went on a basketball and baseball scholarship, but after he got there, the coaches found that he had been an all-conference receiver in football at Lawrenceburg High School. So, even though he was young and turned seventeen the day he started college, the coaches talked him into playing all three sports. As a wide receiver on offense, Dad made All-American football honors at Wharton. He also played the other two sports, and loved the three sports equally.

A young lady named Betty Lou Spellman was also a student at Wharton; she was a member of the dance team called the Starlettes. One day Coach Bahnsen, Dad's basketball coach, came to him and said, "Sonny, I've got a girl picked out for you. She's gorgeous, and I think you'd like to take her out."

That was all the encouragement Dad needed, and before too long they met, fell in love, and became engaged to marry. What they didn't know was that it would be another two and a half years before they would be able to begin their lives together.

After they graduated from junior college, and before their marriage, Mom went to Southwest Texas State College to continue her studies.

Dad, however, didn't follow. Instead, he went to Florida State in Tallahassee, Florida, on a basketball and baseball scholarship. Dad's ambition was to be a major league baseball player. Even though he and Mom were engaged when they separated, the baseball scouts told Dad that he would have a better opportunity of making it in the pros if he was single. He had given up football because at that point he felt that he had the best career possibilities with baseball.

After Dad's first year at Florida State, he visited with his parents, and he received permission to go to Southwest Texas State. At that time his mother said, "We don't care where you receive your education, Sonny. We just want you to be happy, and if Betty is what makes you happy, we're supportive of your decision to transfer. After all, she is a *beautiful* girl."

Dad then moved to San Marcos and began his studies there. He and Mom were finally married on September 4, 1965, a week before Dad's twenty-first birthday. They were married in the Methodist church in El Campo, Texas. Dad's parents, whom I have always called Maw Maw and Paw Paw, gave them a new 1965 Chevrolet Super Sport 396 for a wedding present. Even though the car didn't have air conditioning, they began their marriage in style.

Following their honeymoon in Indiana, my folks drove back to San Marcos and started school there. Dad wanted to become a coach, and they were happy to begin life together. They first lived in a little upstairs three-room apartment, with the bathroom being across the hall. It was on Hopkins Street. They were deeply in love, and life was good.

MY BIRTH

A little over a year after their marriage, my folks were excited to learn that Mom was expecting their first baby—which, as my luck would have it, turned out to be me!

I was born in the Hayes Memorial Hospital on October 30, 1967. Mom had hoped for a girl, and would have named her Kimberly Dee. But Dad was happy because he wanted to have a son to follow in his athletic footsteps. I weighed in at 7 pounds 11 ounces, and was about 20 inches long. Because I was born during the kickoff of Monday Night Football, featuring the Kansas City Chiefs, Dad watched the game in the waiting room while Mom delivered me. Three years later I received my very first football uniform, pads and all. It was a Kansas City Chiefs uniform, and I was the proudest three-year-old in the neighborhood!

Following my birth, it took my folks five days to agree on a name for me. Dad had heard of two high-school-aged brothers in San Marcos who were named Ty and Bo Harrison, and he liked their first names. He thought these names were solid, athletic names, so every day he would "lobby" for the name of Ty, and Mom would think of another name.

The first dignified name they came up with for me was David Hubert, and Dad thought of just nicknaming me Ty. But Mom was against nicknames, so the next day they thought of Troy Hubert as a name. Dad again agreed, and said that he would just call me Ty. By the end of the week, Mom told Dad that if he was insistent on calling me Ty, that would be my name, because she wasn't going to have a son known by a nickname.

In the meantime, while Mom was still in the hospital with me, Dad was home with both sets of grandparents, who had come for my birth. They would call out the different names from their respective rooms, like a hog-calling contest, to see which names sounded best, as though the names had been announced on a loudspeaker system in a college stadium. Dad wanted my name to sound just right, because he had high aspirations for my athletic future, even when I was three or four days old.

They finally agreed on the name of Ty, because it

sounded so *right* to Dad, and they gave me the middle name of Hubert, after my father and grandfather. It was the perfect name for me, and ever since I can remember I have been proud of my name.

At the time of my birth, Dad was playing wide receiver for the San Antonio Toros, a semi-professional football team. He was earning a grand total of fifty dollars per game. He really had great hands, and from all I've been able to learn, that was it—no wheels! But I guess his hands were able to catch about anything that was thrown to him, so he did all right.

I actually attended my first football game when I was two weeks old. Mom took me so she could watch Dad play, and because my grandparents were there, they moved the entire nursery over to the football field so they could indoctrinate me early—and let me see the game in comfort.

As one might expect, one of my very first toys was a football. My dad wanted me to kick it through the wooden pegs in my crib; but as a newborn, I didn't really see myself as a kicker, so I didn't accommodate him. I think he got over it, though, because he would buy me another football whenever he had the chance.

We moved from our home in San Marcos to Bunker Hill Drive in San Antonio when I was a year old. My folks have often said how excited they were to move to their own home and have Dad settle down to a coaching profession.

THE CRIB CAPER

One night, when I was about a year old, my folks put me in my baby bed for the night and then shut the door. They say that when they closed the door I began yelling and screaming and kicking at my bed, wanting to get out. But I decided that wouldn't work, and so I guess I worked my way out of the bed, waddled over to the door, and quietly began to knock.

As Mom remembers it: "Ty showed us, even at that early age, that he was a determined spirit—and that if he really wanted to do something, it would get done. That was the first time he had gotten out of his baby bed, and it surely changed our life-style."

OTHER EARLY SKILLS

Something else happened when I was about a year old. I received a Christmas gift of my first bell-ringing basketball hoop. I got a small basketball to go with it, and I would go down and put the ball right in the basket—my Dad says with "great regularity." He also says this is where I learned to react to crowd approval, since he and Mom always clapped for joy when I hit a basket.

I am told that I was really the center of attention that Christmas, since I was the very first grandchild. Even so, I'm sure I didn't mind.

A NEW LITTLE SISTER—DEE LYN

When I was nineteen months old, my mother gave birth to a new little sister, whom they named Dee Lyn. She was born June 5, 1969, at the Methodist hospital in San Antonio. Mom says that I was pretty jealous of Dee due to the fact that she took my mom away from me. But I just remember feeling good when I was able to hold her.

Mom has told me later that Dee and I were opposite personalities: I was very intense in whatever I wanted to do; Dee, on the other hand, was more laid back, and just went from one activity to another without getting too emotionally involved.

But they tell me that I had quite a temper when I didn't get what I wanted, as the baby bed caper showed. Thank goodness this was worked out of me before my memory began, because I have always displayed perfect manners on the football field (just kidding!). I have worked on it, though, and I think I'm a lot better at controlling my temper now than I was when I was a little boy.

AGE THREE LEADERSHIP OPPORTUNITIES

By the time I was three years of age, I had to learn to baby-sit Dee, and Mom would have me tend her out in the front yard. If Dee left the yard, I would have to run into the house and yell, "Betty"—which is what I called her then—"Dee going down the street!" I was forced into being responsible, even then.

The only problem with this was that years later, when we were teenagers, I still wanted to boss her around because I knew better, and she just didn't want any of it. I never have been able to figure out why.

I've also come to understand that even when I was little I didn't have a regular time that I was supposed to go to bed. Because of how irregular my dad's schedule was, I was allowed to stay up just so I could see him. I'd never see him in the mornings because he'd be gone when I got up—and of course he was never around when I took my nap. But I sure have a lot of memories of playing with him late at night. Then either Mom or Dad would rock me to sleep—either that or they'd let me "drop where I fell." I was pretty casual about life, even then.

One of my other early activities was to be taught by my dad how to throw a ball. I couldn't translate the instructions very well, though, and so I just learned to throw anything I could get my hands on—the silverware, pots and pans, anything. Again Mom continues the story: "One day a neighbor lady came over, and when she saw Ty throwing everything but the kitchen sink in whatever direction he was of a mind to, she said, 'Betty, I don't know what I'd do if I had a child who was that destructive.' I was embarrassed at the time, but now that I see how his football career has gone, I'm glad that I spent my early motherhood years being his servant and picking up for him."

Because my grandparents had moved close to us, we just called Mom and Dad by their first names as a way to keep everyone straight in our conversations. Later, when I was in about the second grade, Mom came to me and told me that she really wanted me to call her Mom, or Mama, or whatever, but that I couldn't call her Betty. I was blonde with blue eyes, she was dark with brown eyes, and because we didn't look alike people would think she was my baby-sitter. So she didn't want that, but wanted to be known as my mother. Dad didn't care what we called him, though, as long as we called him *something,* so to this day I still call him Sonny.

NEIGHBORHOOD PLAY

The one friend I had at that time was Andre Montwill. He was a couple of years older than me, as were most of the other kids in the neighborhood, but we still played together. Andre and I would play all day long, and then when it was time for me to go in, he would take something that was mine and I had to chase him around the cars to get it. I really felt persecuted, but I guess that was my first experience at cutting and weaving in and out of traffic!

But by being the youngest in the neighborhood, I learned a toughness that has stayed with me—out of pure survival. I later learned that when I had a problem with one of the older kids, my mom would want to come out and rescue me. But Dad would hold her back, telling her that I had to learn to fight my own battles. I can't believe that I had a dad who wanted me to get beat up all the time! Seriously, though, I think I did learn a mental toughness, and this has helped me in athletics, since I've never known how to back down.

LEARNING TO THROW THE FOOTBALL

One day I was outside throwing the football with my dad, and I was just goofing off and throwing sidearm. Dad fussed at me and said, "Ty, if you're not going to keep your elbow up, I'm not going to play with you." I didn't believe him, though, and threw the next pass sidearm. But he wasn't kidding. "All right," he said, "I'm going in."

But I coaxed Dad to stay out and play, and I promised him that I would throw it right. From that day on I was always aware of the correct way to throw the ball. Looking back, I now appreciate Dad's ability to stick to a decision and to make me do something right. He really taught me how to not compromise; and that attitude and approach to life have helped me more times than I can even imagine.

RIDING MY FIRST BICYCLE

About the same time I learned to throw a football correctly, my folks gave me a bicycle, and I was really eager to learn to ride it. But I couldn't keep it upright, so Mom spent most of a day holding me upright while I pedaled around and around our circle. By the end of the day, she didn't need to hang on, since I had learned to ride by myself.

When my dad came home, I couldn't wait to show him my new skill, so with him and Mom out watching, I started out. But I was nervous with him observing me, and I couldn't turn. So I just crashed into the curb opposite our driveway.

When they got over to me, all I can remember my

dad saying was: "And you say you taught him how to
ride a bicycle?"

I never did use training wheels. They were for girls,
and I didn't need them. To this day, thanks to my mom
and her dedication, I can still ride a bike. I begged for a
skateboard after that, but because we lived on such a big
hill, my dad would never get me one of those. I don't know
whether it was him or Mom or both who decided it—but
they didn't want to jeopardize my health, so this wasn't a
luxury that I had. But I sure could ride a mean bicycle.

A BROTHER, AT LAST

In the spring of my sixth year, I found out that my
mom was expecting her third baby. One morning I awakened and went to my mother's rocking chair and climbed
onto her lap. I said, "I had a dream last night. I dreamed
that I had a little brother and that we were in the front
yard playing football together."

Sometime later, on July 5, 1973, my little brother,
Koy Dennis, was born. As soon as he was able to crawl,
I had him in the front yard playing football with me. He
would grab my leg and hang on, and it was really fun.
The neighbors said that Koy was the only center they
ever saw who learned to hike his diaper before he could
hike the ball. He was pretty special.

FIRST JOBS

Although as kids we were anything but overworked,
we didn't feel spared, at all. Our main jobs were to load
and empty the dishwasher and to take out the garbage.
That doesn't seem like much now, but at the time it was
a constant pressure. I found out early that it didn't help

to fuss about doing it, so I tried to get my jobs done quickly so I could go out to play.

GRADE SCHOOL YEARS

In 1972, I began kindergarten at the Shenandoah Elementary School. I admit right now that I'm terrible when it comes to cutting paper and doing artistic things with my hands. But one time my teacher, Mrs. Burchard, made us color these paper policemen. We then had to cut them out in sections, and I accidentally cut a leg off. I remember telling her that the leg had torn off, just ripped, and she said, "Ty, don't you lie to me. I can tell that it is cut and not ripped. Don't you ever lie to me again." Well, that was a hard lesson for me to learn, but I don't ever remember lying to the teachers again. I got broken of that real quick.

I really loved kindergarten, and one day when I had to go out of town with my folks I just cried and cried. I couldn't stand to think that I would be missing a day of school.

Speaking of scissors, one day I decided to give Dee a haircut—one of her first. So I cut out a big chunk of her hair and let things go from there. When Mom saw what I had done, she said, "Ty, what on earth have you done!" I was quite indignant, and with a frown on my face I answered, "Well, it was hanging in her eyes." That memory is funny now, because I cut the chunk of hair from off the back of her head!

I can hardly believe it, but this was also the year I started playing golf. My folks had given me a Chi Chi Rodriguez set of clubs for Christmas, and I really thought I was cool. We had a par-three course by our home, and my dad would take me out and let me use my driver on every hole. The holes were a hundred to a hundred and thirty yards long, and I was given a lot of encouragement at that time. I really learned to love the game of golf, even during that early age.

The other thing I remember about kindergarten is that it was the very first time I played on a team. It was a tee-ball team, and because Paw Paw had bought a tee for me to practice with, I could always hit the ball.

We had a father-son day for the team that year, and we had a competition to see who could throw the ball the farthest. They had a line drawn to throw from, and I remember someone telling me that I had to throw the ball high into the air to get it to go far. Well, I wound up and threw the ball into the air, and to my embarrassment the ball landed about five yards in front of me. I was upset about that because I knew that I could throw it much farther if only given another chance.

The fathers threw, too, and Dad threw the ball out of the park, past the lights, and out of sight. He won that contest, and I remember being proud that my dad was such a great baseball player. At the time, he was playing for a county rec team in New Braunfels, Texas, and I just knew that I had the greatest dad in all the world! He also still played city league basketball, so even though he was semi-pro in football, he continued to play all three of his favorite sports.

GIRLS AND TROUBLE

I entered the first grade, and one day I wanted to take some deer antlers to school for show-and-tell. I asked my dad, he agreed, and before long I had a nice set of antlers in a big plastic bag. I showed the antlers to the class, all right, but things didn't go as I had planned, and by the end of the day I was glad to get the antlers home.

When I walked into our home, I said, "We got to

learn all about bugs today." Mom said, "What? What did you say?" I answered her as plainly as I could. "I said that we got to study the bugs that were on the deer horns today—the horns that Sonny gave me." Needless to say, Mom apologized to the teacher for having sent antlers that weren't quite cured but had maggots on them.

I didn't like girls back then, and there was a girl who sat next to me and who always wanted to talk to me. I didn't like sitting by her, but the teacher made me.

One day my teacher left the room to go out and patrol by the bus area, and some of the fifth graders came in to watch our class. One of them stood up in front of the class and said, "Anyone who talks has to come up and put their nose in this circle on the blackboard."

I had never been in trouble before this time because I was pretty quiet. Anyway, this girl who sat next to me said something to me, and I replied by telling her to be quiet or we would get in trouble. Well, the fifth graders heard me say that, and they made us both go up in front of the class and put our noses inside the circles. I couldn't handle the embarrassment, though, and within seconds I started crying. I just felt awful. To this day I can still see the tearstains going down the blackboard. Those were the five longest minutes of my life!

FIRST FOOTBALL TEAM

I also started playing flag football in the first grade. My coaches were Lyn Montgomery, Al Derden, and Dee Keller. These men were my coaches all the way to the sixth grade. My personal goal, those days, was to become a great running back like O. J. Simpson. So my folks bought me a pair of O. J. Simpson shoes, with the orange soles and cleats. They were really neat.

One of the few things I remember about playing that year is something that happened when we were accepting the ball on a kickoff. I was one of the two return men, and the kid next to me got the ball. But instead of running forward with it, he ran backward and got flagged in the end zone for a safety. I was pretty upset, because I figured if he didn't know enough to run forward, he should have let me take the ball.

I was a running back at that time, and I think we actually won a few of our games. This may have been the team I was on when that film (the one they ran after the Heisman announcement) was taken that showed me running for a touchdown.

I also played basketball that year, and even though everybody played just about everywhere on the court, we won either first or second in the league. We played with eight-foot goals, and my memory is that I actually made a few baskets for our team. I remember feeling pretty lucky because we had a basketball standard at home, and with my dad and Paw Paw working with me, I had begun to learn to shoot. The only embarrassing thing about playing basketball that year was our uniforms. I was a little, scrawny thing, and my shirt fit okay, but my shorts were so long I looked as if I were wearing a dress. I tried not to let it bother me, though, and had a good time playing.

One of my goals at this time in my life was to always be better at sports than my sister, Dee. One day my mom decided to have a neighbor give Dee twirling lessons with the baton. I made such a fuss about it that Mom also let me take the same lessons. I only learned enough to be better than Dee, though, and when I had achieved this goal I stopped twirling. I learned that my friends had found out about it, and I didn't want to be teased. So I twirled in the house and never developed this talent further.

When I went into second grade, things got off to a pretty rocky start. One time I was supposed to take a book back to the library, but instead of taking it back to the front desk where I should have taken it, I took it back to the shelf where I had gotten it in the first place.

The librarian gave me a late slip when the book turned up missing, and I told her that I didn't have it. So she sent a slip home to my mom, and she couldn't find the book anywhere. I kept telling Mom that I had already taken it back, so we went into the library together to see if we could find it.

When I restated to the librarian that I had already taken the book back, she really got upset and scolded me. She then went over to the shelf and found it.

Well, Mom and I went home, and I was crying pretty hard. The librarian's name was Miss Crouch, but I cried and said to my mom, "Miss *Grouch* told me I had the book, and I had already turned it in, and it isn't fair." Mom laughed at my attempt at humor, and that made me feel a little better. But at least they knew I was telling the truth, and that was the important thing at the time.

This year was also a pivotal one for me in that I was asked to play quarterback on the football team. I earned this position, according to my mom, because I was the only one who could catch the hike of the ball from the center.

At this stage of my life I really didn't have one sport that I preferred over another. I just loved to play any kind of ball, and I was always supported by my parents and grandparents. By participating in all the sports, I had games several nights a week and on Saturdays, so they were really kept hopping.

I also have to say that school itself was good to me. I enjoyed learning, and my grades were always pretty good, so my folks were pleased. I tried to always finish my homework at school so I could play when I got home.

When I entered the third grade, I became even more involved with my friends that year and with sports. This was my last year playing flag football, and even though we finished in third place it was a fun season. My arm was getting stronger, and I felt more comfortable with getting the ball where I wanted to, even with someone chasing me. It was really a confidence-building year for me.

This was also the year I started pitching on our baseball team. I remember that first day of position tryouts, and because I was late getting to practice the coaches had already finished pitching tryouts. But when I went out on the field, the coach asked if I could pitch. Paw Paw spoke for me, telling them that I could pitch and that he had practiced with me.

A moment later I stood on the mound, did my windup, and threw the ball to the catcher. I could throw the ball faster than the others at that time, except for one other guy who was on one of the other teams. Anyway, the catcher at that moment was the assistant coach. He was closer than normal, and when he caught the ball, it rocked him backward and he sat there and said, "Hey, we've got ourselves a pitcher!" Boy, did that ever make me feel good! I smiled at Paw Paw, he winked back, and I knew it was going to be an exciting season.

BRACES AND SCOUTING

At this time I experienced a lot of unhappiness and pain in that my folks made me start wearing braces on my teeth. I had an overbite, and so I also had to wear the headgear. This consisted of an elastic band behind my head, and wires that came across my cheeks and into my mouth. I had to wear this apparatus twenty-four hours a day, seven days a week, and I hated it. My classmates teased me, and so my self-esteem suffered quite a bit. There were even several days that I gave my folks a hassle about going to school after I first got the braces put on, but my teacher worked with me, and soon I went. My folks gave me a sweater with my football team insignia on it to build my self-esteem. And my teacher,

Miss Robbins, worked with me one-on-one, so pretty soon I was able to deal with having to wear these braces. I reluctantly wore them for almost four years, and then they took them off.

My third grade year was also the year that I became an avid Cub Scout. Unfortunately my enthusiasm lasted for only two weeks because I had to miss many of the pack meetings that year; they interfered with soccer. Looking back, I can see how a heavier commitment to Scouting would have rounded me out in a different way, but at the time all I could think of was soccer, so that's what I stayed with.

THE SHINER DAIRY QUEEN MASSACRE

One time when we were on our way to El Campo to visit my mom's parents, we stopped in Shiner, Texas, for an ice-cream treat. We all ordered our choices, and started eating. Koy ordered a strawberry milk shake, and a few minutes later, before we got back in the car to continue our journey, Mom decided to have a taste of his shake. She did, and Koy became so upset that she had taken part of it that he refused to get back in the car.

So Mom handed Koy's shake to Dee, who was sitting on the little fold-down armrest in the front seat. This meant that Dee now had two drinks to hold, Koy's and her own. I was in the backseat, waiting patiently for Koy to get in the car.

But I was bored, knowing that Mom was trying to pry Koy off the back bumper of the car. So I had Dee turn on every knob she could find—the radio, the windshield wipers, everything. I knew that once Dad started the car, there would be quite a show! Finally, when Dad got into the car, Dee couldn't keep the secret, so she said, "Sonny, do you notice anything?"

This made me furious, so I took both feet and kicked

her in the back. She fell forward, spilling both drinks all over the seat and the floor, and I knew I was in big trouble.

My dad, who is usually pretty calm about things, lost it, and began swatting Dee for having spilled the drinks.

I think I was praying pretty hard about that time, hoping I wouldn't be discovered. But through Dee's tears she told him what had happened, and before long I was being dragged out of the car.

I should mention at this point that at home whenever I needed to be spanked (which honestly wasn't that often), Dad would take me into a private room and give me the back of his hand on my backside. Now, with the milk shake running all over the front seat, he took me into the men's room of the Dairy Queen and gave me the paddling I deserved. I knew he couldn't get me to cry, though, so I just took it as it was handed out, and then went out and sat on one of the benches.

By this time, Mom had let Koy go and was running back and forth, getting towels to clean off the front seat of the car. Dad then took Koy into the men's room and gave him what I thought would be a smaller dose of what he had given me, for being upset that Mom had taken a little sip of his milk shake in the first place. Meanwhile, Dee had run into the ladies' room and locked the door, standing in fear of getting the next spanking.

When Dad finished with Koy, he found out where Dee was. So he went to that door, while Mom was still cleaning things up, and yelled, "Dee, open the door . . . I'm not going to spank you. I'm not going to spank you . . . Open the door." Meanwhile, a lady was standing there, wanting to use the rest room, so Dad was even more anxious. Dee finally unlocked the door and came out, then walked quickly to the safety of Mom's skirt and the car.

Things finally did get calmed down, and in a few minutes we were in the car, driving out of town. We had all been told to keep quiet—but Koy couldn't contain himself, and he suddenly blurted, "I'm thirsty! I didn't get anything to drink, and I'm thirsty!"

Needless to say, no one answered him.

But that was sure a long ride to El Campo, all of us having barely survived what we have come to remember as the "Shiner Dairy Queen Massacre."

CONTINUING WITH SCHOOL

The fourth grade began, and I was excited because I knew we would be playing tackle football rather than just flag football. Dad had been coaching at three different schools during this time, and even though I was still in grade school, I liked to follow what was happening with his teams and to sense the excitement of high school ball. He had been assistant coach at South San Antonio High School and assistant coach at Churchill High School—and finally he became the head coach at Somerset High School.

We were the best team in the league that year, taking first place. That gave us big heads, and we thought that we were the tough guys from then on. That year I threw several touchdowns, kicked off for the team, and played safety on defense.

This was also when I began playing basketball for the Catholic league, as well as the YMCA league. That kept me busy, but I really enjoyed it. We took the championship in the Catholic league, and second in the other, so I felt pretty good about that.

I had an experience in golfing during the summer of that year that I'll always remember. My dad had bought my little brother, Koy, and me a summer pass at the course. So we went out and played almost daily. Mom usually dropped us off early in the morning. Even though Koy was only going into kindergarten, he had a little bitty driver and was getting used to the game. One day we became so involved with our playing that we had finished fifty-four holes before we realized what time it was. The thing I remember about this day was seeing Koy drag his set of clubs down the fairways. We were both pretty tired by the time we went home for dinner.

Entering the fifth grade was an important time for me because it meant that I could take Koy to school with me. But our folks had decided to have Koy go to another school, and this upset me quite a bit. So I went to Mom, with tears in my eyes, to plead with her. I told her that this would be the only time in our lives that we could go to the same school, so she and Dad discussed it and finally let Koy go to school with me. It was a great year for that reason, and I'll always remember being responsible for him when we would walk to and from school.

During my fifth grade football season, our team flew up to Dallas and played a team from there. My teacher was pretty supportive of the trip, since I kept up with my schoolwork. (I always competed academically with another kid, whose name was Robert Elliott. At one time we both had several 100 percent test scores in a row, and he finally just took the lead—probably because I was in sports, and he wasn't. Still, with him as a friendly motivator, I received really good grades.) Anyway, we flew up to Dallas for this game, and this was my first time on an airplane, so I was excited. My dad gave us some travel bags, since he was the head coach at Somerset at this time. We beat the Dallas team pretty badly, and this gave us the championship for our age group. As a young quarterback, this was my biggest game to date, and I was pleased with how the team pulled together for the win.

During basketball season, I again played for two different teams. We had nicknames at this time, too. One guy, who was the tallest on the team, was called "Skywalker." My name was "Downtown," and I liked that because the name meant that I was a pretty good shot, even from as far away as "downtown." We had connections with a sporting goods store, and so we wore the best Nike high-tops and top-of-the-line socks, and we all had the same warm-ups and uniforms. They even put our nicknames on the back of our warm-ups, so I had the name Downtown on mine. We really thought we were cool.

I also earned my first B on my report card during this school year. The subject was math, and it was the year that I learned not to like math so much. I kept after it, though, and never did give up.

My mom says this is the year that I "fell in love" for the first time, with a girl named Jenny. But evidently she didn't seem too impressed, so I guess the feelings were just mine.

MIDDLE SCHOOL AT HOBBY

Sixth grade, for me, was a new step since we went into the middle school at that time. The school was called Hobby Middle School, and most of the kids from all of my growing-up teams went there. This was when the popularity craze kicked in, and even though I had been kind of a "big shot" in my elementary school, here I became quite average. I wasn't into all the fashions in what I wore, because I just wouldn't wear the Izod logo on my shirts. I also wouldn't wear my hair as long as the other guys, or cater to being in a popular group, so I became quite average.

My mom could see the hurt on my face, at times, because my friends were changing; but I felt good because I was being the kind of person I wanted to be. Looking back, this was when I learned to reject peer pressure and to be my own person. Not that I thought of myself as being better than the others; I just wanted to feel that I was the same person I had always been, and that others would accept me for that choice.

This year in football I continued as quarterback, and

again we were fortunate to win the league championship. Nothing really extraordinary happened other than that, but it was a great fall season for us.

Basketball season came along, and this time we finished fourth at state. We played in Waco for the tournament, and there was one big black kid who was 6 feet 4 inches tall. That was something for a sixth grader. Anyway, he was playing against us for third place, and he could dunk the ball, while the rest of us just watched in awe with open mouths.

Late in the game, this big guy got a breakaway, and I was the guard that followed him down the court. But I didn't want him to dunk the ball, so I just kind of climbed up his back and hit the ball away. We both fell down, and as he was getting up he scolded, "Now, why do you want to do that? I was going to dunk!" I could see that he was pretty angry, so I just walked away. The last thing I wanted was a fight with *him*.

But the thing I remember about this game was that, even at that early age, I had the competitive spirit. I just had to win in everything I did!

MOM'S BROTHER, UNCLE JON

One of my favorite memories was going to El Campo to my grandparents' house. My mother's younger brother, Jon, was just nine years older than me, and he was always doing fun things with us during those holidays. He would tease us a lot, too, so we never were sure what was going to happen. We just knew that with Uncle Jon *something* was going to happen!

LORI LEA'S BIRTH

This year was exciting for our family in another way, too. Mom was expecting her fourth baby, and on February 28, 1980, my youngest sister, Lori Lea, was born. She just missed being a leap-year baby by a few hours. The three of us kids thought she was the most beautiful baby in the world! I really enjoyed having her in our home and taking care of her.

TRANSITION TO SCHOOL SPORTS

My seventh grade year arrived, and so my experience in playing school sports began. When football season started that fall, we had so many different players that they organized us into two separate teams. We probably had a hundred players come out, and so we had a purple team and a gold team. I was on the gold team, which was equally balanced with the purple team.

I started this season as first-string defensive safety, while being second-string quarterback. This was quite an adjustment for me, because up until this time I had always been first-string quarterback. So when practices would start I found myself goofing off more and more, and I was really beginning to get a poor attitude. I didn't really pay attention to the offensive coordinator, and as a result I really didn't learn the offense as I should have.

I did work hard on defense, though, and would get quite a few interceptions, and forced myself to excel to my potential.

Both of our teams were undefeated that year, and so even though I slipped a bit offensively, still I was quite happy with my defensive efforts.

Basketball season then began, and I was lucky to find myself playing first-string guard for the team. Our coach, Mr. Dry, was great, and I really liked the way he coached. He was totally positive, a people builder. What he taught me about myself and about reaching for my potential was important and has stayed with me ever since.

I also have to say how much it meant to have my family support me by always showing up when I played. Maw Maw and Paw Paw, as well as my mother, would always attend, and Dad would come whenever he wasn't coaching his own teams. Mom would also bring Dee and Koy, and so my games were pretty much a family-support affair. Even though Koy was six years younger than I, he had a knack for athletics and was pretty intense for a kid his age. He was just beginning his organized sports activities, actually, and it was fun to encourage him and to see him develop with his skills.

This was also a year of change for me, due to the growing difference between me and some of my life-long friends. I just couldn't force myself to get caught up in the popularity contests, and I found that my values and the way I had been taught to conduct myself were becoming quite different from the values and behavior of many of my friends. I don't want to sound critical of them, since I didn't consider myself any better than they were, but things just weren't the same between us.

This wasn't really a fun year for me, all the way around. My friends seemed to want other things in life and were caught up in the social scene, so I let my grades suffer, as well. I even managed to pull myself down to getting B's and C's in some of my classes, and I found myself struggling to get excited about even going to school.

One of my most embarrassing moments took place during my seventh grade year. One day after participating in P.E. and changing clothes, I found that I was late for my next class. I ran back to my locker and threw my things into it. It wasn't really an organized locker, and so I just stuffed things into it. I was running to class with my notebook, and four or five of the really popular girls were coming out of the double doors about the same time. There was a crack in the floor and my toe caught it, sending me flying! My notebook went everywhere, and I just slid for about twenty feet, like sliding into home plate in baseball.

I rubbed all of the red paint off the snaps on the red windbreaker I was wearing, and when I looked up I was right at the feet of these girls. Was I ever embarrassed! I had to get up and pick up all my papers, and then walk by them, and I've never been so happy to get out of a place in my life.

One day during practice my football coach called me over to him and said, "Ty, do you know why you're not starting at quarterback?" I was surprised at his question, and I said, "Because I'm not fast enough?" He answered slowly. "Well," he said, "we just want someone to start for us who is a little bit stronger and tougher, and who is a little bit bigger than you are."

That was a difficult conversation for me to have, and I went home and told my dad what the coach had said. We then talked about my possibly repeating the seventh grade so that I could catch up, maturity-wise. I told him at the time that I really didn't want to stay back, but instead wanted to continue along into the eighth grade with my friends.

The day before my eighth grade school year was to begin, we went out and had a practice. The two quarterbacks from the year before picked up a ball and started warming up, and another kid and I also picked up a ball and started throwing it to each other. This lasted until the coaches came out onto the field. They told the other kid and me to put the ball down, and then instructed the other boys to continue throwing.

This moment had a profound effect on my emotions, and I left practice that day determined to talk to Dad about my feelings. I called him when I got home and told him that I felt the coaches were playing favorites, and that I wanted to consider staying back in the seventh grade so that I could play. Being a coach himself, Dad didn't want to hear about how I was being treated, so he just said that we could talk about it when he got home.

Sometime later, Dad arrived. We sat down with Mom and really got to the point. Dad really quizzed me, and asked, "Are you really sure you want to do this, Ty?" "Yessir," I answered, "I really am. I want a chance to play quarterback, and I know I'm not going to get to do it at Hobby."

Dad was coaching at Central Catholic High Schoool at this time, which was a private high school. Anyway, he talked with my school officials, and they said that I couldn't stay back in seventh grade in the public school system, because I hadn't failed that grade. So this made my decision for me, and I enrolled in a private school—Mount Sacred Heart for Boys—which was a Catholic school that was administered by several nuns.

Talk about an adjustment! We had to wear military uniforms and had to march from class to class; I'd never been involved in anything like that before. But my parents and grandparents encouraged me, telling me that I had to live with my decision, and so I worked hard to make things work.

To my surprise, life actually began to be fun again. I got in with a new group of friends who had similar values, and my grades went back up to A's.

At Mount Sacred Heart, the seventh and eighth grade football players were combined for one team because there weren't enough of them to field two teams; so I began to work out with the other quarterback, who was by now in the eighth grade. He knew the option plays, which was what they ran there, so I started at middle linebacker.

The first day out, the coaches didn't know who was going to play linebacker. They did have one player who was pretty big, and they knew he was going to play. Still, they couldn't find another one, so they asked me what position I had played in the public school system. I told them I had played defensive safety. Their response was to tell me that I was a little bit big for a safety in this league, and that they wanted me to play linebacker.

I agreed, and finally the first game began. For the first play from the line of scrimmage, we were on defense. They handed off to their running back, who came right toward me. I was pretty excited, and I hit him right in the stomach with my helmet, knocking the wind out of him. He also fumbled the ball, and we were on our way.

This tackle really impressed the coaches, so they said I was to be a linebacker for sure.

The season finally ended, and I found that I had made the all-star team as defensive linebacker. But this wasn't all. Whenever we got into a passing situation, they would let me go in as quarterback and pass the ball. They saw that I could pass quite well and get the ball to the receivers, so this was an added bonus because all I really wanted to do was play quarterback.

I really appreciated the nuns, too, who were my teachers. They would let me get ahead and work at my own pace. So without too much effort I was back into getting straight A's. I should have gotten good grades, though, since this was my second year to be in the seventh grade.

School was really starting to be fun again, and my confidence came back quite easily. I wasn't used to wearing khaki and maroon uniforms, but at least I didn't have to pick out my clothes every morning; my decision was made for me.

This disciplined environment was a blessing for me in another way, too. During this time drug use was really setting into the public middle school where I had attended. At Mount Sacred Heart I was able to stay away from that environment and keep my life focused. I just found that it conformed more to the type of person I wanted to be, so I was really happy to be there.

This Catholic school also gave me a chance to learn a little more about other religions, especially the Catholic church. My friends weren't perfect, and sometimes they would do crazy things. But they always participated in what they called "confession," in which they confessed their sins and started over. I was tempted to do this a time or two, but I never did go to confession, since I wasn't Catholic.

But one time I did take communion with the others, and that experience felt good, even though I did it more out of curiosity than anything else. A wafer was placed in my mouth by the sister. I knew I was supposed to say something, but I didn't know the right words, so I just took it and held it in my mouth as I walked back to my seat. I asked the kid I was sitting next to what I should do with it. He told me to eat it, so I did. This was during a dress-up mass service with the girls, who attended a similar school across the fence from our own.

I have to say that I had participated in communion before this at the Methodist church, and those had been good monthly experiences for me. They served bread and grape juice, and I had always gone up, knelt down, and taken that.

The seventh and eighth grades were also combined for the basketball teams, and so I played guard on that team and had a fun time. My nickname changed that year to "Dr. D," which stood for "Dr. Dunk." I couldn't dunk the ball, but that was a cool name, so I gladly accepted it.

I was learning to shoot pretty well, too, and one game I even scored thirty points. But there was also the time that I shot an air ball, and that really took the wind out of my sails. I knew I wasn't hot, so I cooled it and passed off to the others for the rest of that game.

When we finally got to the championship game, we played a team that had two very good brothers on it. This team was always the one to beat.

The game was almost over—in fact, there was just one

second left. I was shooting a one-and-one at the foul line, and this was the first time I had been in a pressure situation where the game was a tie, with the win depending on me.

We were playing on their home court, so the crowd was screaming and my mind was really struggling to concentrate on the shot. I was thinking of how my dad had always taught me to put the ball right over the front of the rim, and how I had become pretty good at doing just that.

I was about to shoot when a really funny feeling came over me, and I felt a big choke coming on. I bounced the ball a couple of times, looked at the basket, and then let the ball fly. But I didn't follow through with my shot, and the ball barely hit the front of the rim.

Needless to say, we then went into overtime. I was really upset, too, because during overtime a couple of our good players fouled out. We ended up losing the game by a couple of points in double overtime, and I felt bad because I knew I could have won it for us at the end of regulation play.

When we were on our way home, Dad turned to me and said, "Well, Ty, now that you've been in that situation, it won't happen again. You will have been there before, and you will know how to block out your mind and put the ball in the basket. It's a good lesson to learn and to get over with now, because you won't let it happen again."

I'll have to say that ever since then, whenever I have been in that game-winning situation, I have been able to make the basket. It really was a good lesson for me to learn because afterwards I was always able to calm down, block the crowd from my mind, and take the proper shot.

Even though we didn't win that championship, I did make the all-tournament team. I probably would have made MVP if I hadn't choked at the foul line, but I guess that's the way we learn.

It was that school year, with the private girls' school across the fence from us, that I learned about girls. The guys were crazy about girls, and they would tape notes to the bottom of Frisbees or tie them to rocks, and do anything to break the rules and talk to the girls during school hours. They had a lot of fun, but I was too shy, so I just laughed along with them without doing anything about it myself.

I really think that year was the turning point in my life, since I learned that I could succeed without succumbing to peer pressure, and that I could determine my own level of achievement.

OUR MOVE TO LAREDO

As fall approached, Dad received a coaching job a hundred and fifty miles southwest of San Antonio in Laredo, Texas, on the Mexico border. So we packed our things and moved out there. We moved from a four-bedroom home to a single-wide mobile home, and because we had stored most of our belongings in Maw Maw and Paw Paw's garage, we set off on our adventure. This was a pretty hard year, especially for Mom.

I entered the eighth grade at this time, attending the United Middle School, which then fed into United High. My dad was coaching at Martin High, but we lived in the other area, so I attended school there.

This was the first year they played tackle football, but because I had already played it, this gave me an advantage. So I was named the starting quarterback, and I was eager to prove myself.

I was eager, that is, until we lost our first game 7-0 to Eagle Pass. The thing that upset me was that I had thrown a pass to a receiver on a corner route, and he caught it and ran a big circle instead of just going straight. Because of this, he stepped on the out-of-bounds line. He would have scored, but he didn't.

I made friends quickly among the players at United because I knew how to put the pads in the uniform pants, and the others didn't have a clue as to how to do it. So I helped them, and suddenly they thought I was pretty cool. But I had played tackle for four years, so it was no big deal for me—even though I didn't say that to them.

I missed the person-to-person atmosphere of the private Catholic school, but I jumped right in and made a lot of friends. This made the adjustment an easy one. Mom and Dad had challenged us kids to do this, and even though it was easy for Koy, Dee and I had to set our minds to it, and before long we fit right in.

GRANDDAD SPELLMAN'S DEATH—1983

My mom's parents, Alva Hartman and Clyde Spellman, lived almost their entire lives in El Campo, Texas. This is a small town about seventy miles southwest of Houston, near Victoria.

Granddad was a big golfer, and would play an entire round, including putting, with just the "one" iron. He was only 5 feet 9 inches tall, but was strong and broad shouldered, so he always seemed big to me. As a chiropractor with an office beside his home, he could pretty much leave and go golfing whenever he was of a mind to.

So, while we were living in Laredo, we received word from my mom's sister that Granddad, at age sixty-nine, had passed away of a heart attack. Because his death was sudden, we weren't able to be there. But we packed our things, drove all the way to El Campo, and attended the funeral. Granddad had been born nearby in Rocky, Texas. He was buried in the family cemetery mentioned earlier.

That was a very hard time for me, since I had been so close to both him and my grandmother. Granddad had always kept a garden out back of his house, and even though I didn't really like to eat the vegetables, still I loved going out and picking the cucumbers, green beans, or whatever was needing to be picked at the time.

Granddad's greatest quality was his patience. He was a joker, and was always telling us a joke about something. But what I remember about him more than his happy nature is his kindness and patience. Largely because of his example, I have tried to become a patient person—although at times on the ball field I forget patience when a receiver runs a wrong route, a lineman doesn't block correctly, and so forth. My grandmother tells me that I've also inherited Granddad's inclination to be a jokester.

My grandmother, on the other hand, was an Avon representative. Some of us grandkids called her Grandma Avon because of all the Avon gifts she would give us. She also loved to play cards, and would play all night long if she could get someone to stay up and play with her. We would play Yahtzee, canasta, and other games whenever we went to her home for a holiday or on vacation. These memories with my mom's parents are some of the happiest of my youth.

BACK TO SCHOOL AND SPORTS

This first game was the only one we lost that year, so football was really fun again. And because I was finally the starting quarterback, I felt that I could do about anything. I started throwing a lot, and I remember throwing quite a few touchdown passes. It was more fun than I had known in a long time.

Basketball season then began, and I played guard, with Coach Gonzales becoming a good friend. I was named MVP in the tournament that year, and because I had quite long arms, I began to block shots and play pretty good defense.

MOVING BACK TO SAN ANTONIO

Toward the end of my eighth grade year, my dad was hired back in San Antonio, this time as head coach at Southwest High School. So we moved back, where I finished the school year.

A lot of folks have asked if I felt that I was at a disadvantage, with our family moving around as often as we did. To be honest, I saw it as an advantage. Dad didn't have the security of coaching at the good, big schools. Instead, he had to coach out on the fringe where the programs needed a lot of help. As a result, he had to always be learning new defenses and figuring out how to beat the other teams.

I think this became a blessing for me. I began to read defenses like walking in my sleep, and this skill would not have been developed if Dad hadn't changed coaching jobs several times.

Dad was also considered a maverick, because whereas all the other teams ran the ball, Texas-style, Dad liked to throw it! He had been a wide receiver, as I have said, and so he knew how to win with that kind of game plan.

That summer, as I prepared to enter high school and to move up a notch in the caliber of athletics that were played, I had no idea how much impact my father, as the varsity head football coach, would have in my life to come. So I enjoyed the summer golfing with Koy and with my friends. We also fished a lot, and in general became accustomed to living back in San Antonio. But even though I was thoroughly enjoying my summer vacation, I was anxious to begin my high school career.

High School Years in Texas

MY FRESHMAN YEAR

When my freshman year began at Southwest High School, we had a pretty good team, and went undefeated. My favorite receiver was Kevin Jennings, who was a gifted athlete.

That previous spring, when we moved back to San Antonio from Laredo, we had to live within our district boundaries in order for me to be eligible to play ball there. Because our home was out of the district, we rented it out that year, while renting another home for ourselves within the district. We lived on a street named Turkey Flat, and I sure didn't want my friends to know the name of that street.

DRUGS AND ALCOHOL

Another thing I encountered after moving back to San Antonio was the heavy use of drugs among young people there. The kids my age were experimenting, more than anything else, but it was there, and it affected many of them. When I turned sixteen, I received my driver's license. My friends then assigned me to be the driver when we would go to parties, since they would drink. Their parents even called me "Father Ty" because it was my job to be responsible in getting them home.

Either my friends didn't know enough to leave alcohol alone, or else they just wanted to rebel. So I took it upon myself to help keep them out of trouble. I knew how to have fun without drinking, so this wasn't even an issue with me. I wasn't trying to be a hero or anything like that. I just didn't want any of them to get in an accident or to hurt somebody.

BACK TO SPORTS—MINE AND MY DAD'S

Getting back to my freshman year of athletics, our basketball team again went undefeated for the season. Many of the guys from the football team also played basketball, and because we were all in pretty good shape, we pressed a lot and did the fast break whenever we could.

When spring arrived, my dad was having some difficulties with the front office at Southwest, and he thought he would be leaving the school. The administration hadn't been very cooperative with purchase orders and other things he needed for the football program, so he thought he would be coaching somewhere else. As a result of this situation, I transferred to Clark High School to finish out my freshman year.

Because Clark was a 5-A school, they had spring football; so I went through this spring practice thinking I would go either there the following year or to wherever my dad was coaching. I played quarterback as well as safety, although I shared the positions with the others who had already been on the team.

Toward the end of spring ball, Dad worked things out

with the administration, and he would be coaching again at Southwest. This meant that I wouldn't be going to Clark, after all, since we had all looked forward to my playing for his teams. Dad had always been the one to teach me the little lessons about respect and loyalty, so when this awkward situation came up, he told me that I needed to go up and ask the head coach at Clark if I could still play in the spring game and at the same time indicate to him that I wouldn't be attending that school in the fall.

I did as Dad suggested, and the coach still allowed me to play some in the spring game, even though he was trying out the players he would be using that next season. I think he appreciated my being open and honest with him.

BEING A MIGHTY SOPHOMORE

Before school began that fall, we had two-a-day football practices, and I received my first real introduction to my dad as my coach. I was excited about the opportunity of playing for varsity, due to the fact that so many of the former team members had graduated. Because of this, we knew that we would have a young team, and my playing situation looked quite good.

As things turned out, I was named the starting quarterback and played along with five or six other sophomores in the lineup.

Because our team was so young, we ended the season with a 3-6-1 record. This wasn't too good, but it was a building year for the team, and I had a great time playing for my dad. He brought us along slowly, and didn't put any more pressure on me than he did anyone else.

This season taught me some good lessons, too. Even though we didn't win too often, Dad would keep our motivation and morale up, giving us a good team spirit.

Our school hadn't been to the play-offs in twenty-five years—so it was really a building year. We knew that if we worked hard and kept in shape during the off season, we'd have a good shot at the league championship the following year.

By this time I was about 5 feet 10 inches tall and weighed 145 pounds. That wasn't too big, but I made it through the season. In fact, in my best game I was nine out of ten in passing for 150 yards. These weren't great stats, but I did gain a lot of confidence by it.

This was also the first year I really learned to read defenses, so my knowledge of the quarterback duties had moved up several notches. I learned to pick up the hot receiver on blitzes and to make reads when I dropped back to pass. The biggest challenge for me was standing in the pocket during a pass rush by the defense. This was the first time I had experienced that kind of pressure, and it was not an easy thing to learn patience under those high-intensity rushes.

To put this season in perspective, this was the time period I learned the most about football. I also participated in basketball, baseball, track, and golf.

In basketball, my friends and I played on the junior-varsity team. We went on a lot of road trips and to several tournaments. I played guard and forward, and because we pressed and ran, I had a couple of thirty-point games. I averaged somewhere in the twenties, so I had a lot of fun.

At the end of the season, the varsity team earned the right to go to the play-offs. Because of this, a couple of us got called up to be on the varsity for the remaining games in the season. Kevin Jennings and I were the players who had this opportunity. He and I even got into the games when they were pretty well won by the starters.

The highlight for me was when we won our zone play-off game, and I even made six or seven points toward the end. It was an overtime game, and because the man defending me kept fouling, I was lucky enough to be able to shoot foul shots. They were clutch free throws, but because of what my dad had taught me before, I was able to concentrate and have the attitude of making the shots. It worked, too, so he must have been right.

Baseball, track, and golf were all held at the same time, of course, and even though I was never really serious about track, I participated in it to keep in shape for football. I ran the 330-meter intermediate hurdles in the junior-varsity meets rather than in the varsity competition, so I didn't letter in track that year.

My schedule was pretty hard, actually. I would work out at the track for about an hour and a half while varsity baseball practice was also going on. I would then leave the track and go up to the baseball field, where I would be one of the last to take batting and fielding practice. I was fortunate to be a starter at third base, or would play shortstop or second base, depending on who was pitching. We went to the play-offs that year but lost during the first round.

Golf, for me, was just a day out of school. We had one tournament, and I shot about ninety for the eighteen-hole tournament, so it was just something fun to do. The reason why I lettered in that sport was that we only had two golfers on the team. So it wasn't really a golf *team,* just a golf *duo!*

The summer between my sophomore and junior years was spent moving back into our own home on Bunker Hill. We had been forced to live within the district boundaries for only one school year, after which we could live where we wanted while I continued to attend school at Southwest.

I also spent the summer going to school every other day and working out. Medina River ran right next to our practice field, so we'd go down there and catch catfish after we'd worked out. We also set trotlines in the evening, and then would go back the next morning and

check them out. Our family really enjoyed eating fish, so
this was good sport.

A FUN JUNIOR YEAR

There was a lot of anticipation in the air as we began
our two-a-days preceding my junior year at Southwest.
There were quite a few young players coming back, and
Dad convinced us that we could do some great things if
we set our minds to it. I had been actively lifting weights
for two years by this time, and I felt that Coach Lehman,
our line and strength coach, was helping me quite a bit
in this area. He and Dad had played together for the
Toros in the semi-pros, and I really liked him.

By this time I was about 5 feet 11 inches tall and
weighed 150 pounds. This meant I had put on a lot of
weight during the past year—five full pounds! Seriously, I
did work hard, but for some reason the additional weight
has always been slow in coming.

The season finally began, and our first game was
against another rival, the Medina Valley Panthers. They
had beaten us the previous nine years.

Before the game began, my dad joked with me and
said, "Ty, let's go out and throw for two hundred." He
laughed when he said it, and I thought he was kidding,
because I had never thrown for over 150.

But we went out with a good mental set, and I was
ready to prove myself. As an added bonus, we had a
little tight end, Dennis Ray, who was a full 5 feet 6
inches tall and who weighed a hefty 140 pounds. He was
our ace, since he was deceptively fast. For a tight end,
Dennis was like lightning. He would always outrun his
defenders, so I was able to throw quite a few long bombs
to him. We also had Herman Loving as a fullback, and
he was probably 5 feet 10 inches tall, weighing 200
pounds. Herman would just run over people. If he had

an open field, he wouldn't put a move on—he'd just run over the defensive player who was trying to tackle him. Darrell Davis was our halfback, and he was just a sophomore at 6 feet 2 inches, weighing about 185 pounds. He was a big-time running back with good size, good speed, and great moves. All three of these guys complemented each other, and could they ever play!

We had two great outside receivers: Mario Laque, who didn't have great speed but had super hands, and would catch anything thrown in his direction; and my good friend Kevin Jennings, who had speed plus savvy with the routes he ran and who had also been blessed with great hands.

So this group was awesome. Out of all of us, only Mario and Dennis were seniors, so Dad felt good about our long-term success as a team.

Anyway, the game began with us on defense. Unfortunately, our defense let them move right on down the field and score a touchdown. It looked like the same old thing as in years past, but I knew if we could play to our potential offensively, we were ready to give them a battle.

When they kicked off to us, we ran a trick play right off the bat. We received, and for this play I was on the kickoff return team. I wasn't way back to receive, but I was there, waiting.

We returned the ball to the right, and our return man got tackled. I was just milling around, fixing my shoelace while the referee spotted the ball. Meanwhile, everybody else was lining up over on the other side of the field. Darrell and a couple of other guys were in the backfield, and I got down over the ball and snapped it sideways.

At that instant the defense was yelling, "Over there! Over there!" but by then it was too late, since Darrell had gotten the ball from me and was heading down the field. He went about sixty yards on that play, and was finally tackled on the twenty-yard line. On the next play I hit Dennis Ray on a pass across the middle, and he ran it in for a touchdown. We matched them score for score from then on. Dennis caught another touchdown for about eighty yards, and then another for about seventy yards. His great offensive play, in addition to the two or three interceptions he had on defense, gave him a career day. He couldn't have been more happy, and I was happy for him.

The final score was 35-28 in our favor, and were we ever excited! I had thrown for 350 yards and several touchdowns, and I was really pleased with how well we all had played.

One of the local TV stations had just started a high school highlight reel on Sunday mornings, recapping the games and scores. That Sunday morning when the program began, I was named Player of the Week for the San Antonio schools. Dad told me that no Texas quarterback had ever thrown for that many yards in a high school game before, since the coaching philosophy had been to run the ball—three yards and a cloud of dust. Needless to say, I was pretty happy with how well the game had gone.

This win allowed us to start off the season on a good foot, and we just kept winning from there. We played Carizzo Springs High toward the middle of the season, with both of us having identical 4-0 records going into the game. They were from the south zone and we were from the north, so it was a great rivalry. We knew that regardless of the outcome of the game, we would very likely meet them again in the play-offs.

The game finally ended with our team coming out on top 28-14. It was a tough game, but we had better athletes than they did, and we finally wore them down. This was probably our biggest win to date because they were so highly rated.

By the time we had finished our ninth game, we were undefeated and were crowned district champs. We then had our homecoming week and were scheduled to play South San West Campus, just down the street from us.

Thursday night before the game, we had a bonfire and pep rally, with the entire team attending. Afterward, some of the players decided to go over and drive around the West Campus. They had been drinking, and a couple of them had taken drugs, so they weren't in very good shape.

When these guys arrived on the campus, the West Campus girls' volleyball team had just left practice, and they saw our players' cars circling the school. So they got in their cars and tried to get out of the parking lot. But they were stopped by our guys' cars. One of our linebackers, who was intoxicated, pulled one of the girls out of the car she was in and, I'm sorry to say, began beating her up. He was not only our starting linebacker but also all-district—a real star. Pretty soon the police arrived, and things were handled.

The next morning my dad called us all out of our classes and told us that because of what happened, we might not be going to the play-offs. He later called those guys out who had been involved in the incident, one by one, and dismissed them from the team. He said we might have to forfeit the game because there was so much bad blood between the schools.

Later that day, the other coach talked with Dad, and they decided to play the game after all. They did this because of our season, and the fact that this was the first time in twenty-five years that we had made the play-offs. His reasoning was that we didn't all have to suffer because of the actions of a few.

The school officials decided to let us go ahead and play the game at a neutral site. They postponed it until the next day, which was a Saturday, and we played it in the afternoon. That made our homecoming anti-climactic, but it was better than not playing at all.

The suspension of players from our team meant that we had to start a couple of freshmen on defense. This factor really hurt because we hadn't been that good on defense in the first place. Still, we were pretty determined, and we won the game 48-20, to go undefeated through the final regular-season game.

With a record of 10-0, we went to the play-offs. And, as we had expected, we were assigned to play Carizzo Springs in the first round. We were all excited because we had been the only team to beat them during the regular season. We flipped a coin and they won the toss, so we went to their school to play the game.

Carizzo Springs was three hours southwest of San Antonio, so we had a long bus ride to get there. We stopped to rest part way there, and Dad was so excited that he got out and put Southwest Dragon signs on the tree trunks and anywhere else he could think of. He was really working on our minds. It was fun to see him get so excited because I was used to seeing him be pretty loose at home. But he was fired up just as if he were one of the players, and that was fun to see.

We continued our journey, and all of us were thinking of the Carizzo Springs rough-tough-guy image. They really intimidated their opposition. In fact, when opposing teams would drive into their stadium, their seniors would be sitting on the steps where the bus would stop and would try to intimidate the visiting team.

My dad had known of this intimidation factor, so he asked Herman and Dennis to get up in front of the bus with the instruction that Herman, at 200 pounds, run out of the bus chasing Dennis, at 140 pounds—and that Herman catch Dennis, pin him down, and start beating on him. He said that would distract the Carizzo Springs players, and give the psychological advantage to us.

So this is what happened. The bus stopped, the bus doors sprung open, and Dennis took off with Herman chasing him. We all piled out of the bus and started yelling, "Get him, Herman!" and things like that. Herman finally caught Dennis over by the ticket gate, and began beating on him as Dad had instructed him to do.

The Carizzo Springs players were laughing and patting themselves on the back, since they could see that we didn't have our minds on the game. They hurried in and retrieved the rest of their players from their locker room so that they could watch. Now both teams were distracted, which, from where we stood, made us about even.

Dad finally broke up the so-called fight, and before long we were dressed and ready for the game to begin.

We won the coin toss and elected to receive. Darrell received the ball, ran first to the right, then back to the left, and was finally tackled in our end zone for a safety. They were now ahead 2-0.

We then kicked off to them, and about six plays later they scored a touchdown, making the score 9-0. About that time we were all wondering just how good this staged-fight plan of Dad's had been. Meanwhile, Dad was going up and down the sidelines saying, "It's going to take forty-five points to win anyway, so just keep your heads up and we'll be all right."

On the next series I threw a tight end throw-back screen to Dennis Ray, and he went about eighty yards for a touchdown. That sort of equalized things, and we settled down to play ball.

With about two minutes left in the game, we were ahead 44-36. Then, a minute later, they were driving down at about our thirty-yard line. If they scored and then went for two extra points and got them, we would be tied on the scoreboard. The game would then go to the team with the most penetrations—penetrations being the number of times a team advances to inside the opponent's twenty-yard line. We were tied on that statistic. We were also tied on first downs, so it would be very difficult to determine a winner in that case.

At that point, our free safety, Carl Roberson—a gifted runner who was about 6 feet 4 inches tall and who weighed 220 pounds—made a great play. He saw the ball coming on a potential touchdown pass, and he leaped up, intercepted it cleanly, and then outran the opponents for about a ninety-yard touchdown. We won by a score of 51-36.

It was an incredible game, and was probably one of the better high school games that had been played in the state of Texas. In that game I was fortunate enough to break the state single-season passing record for 4-A ball.

The next game we played New Braunfels Canyon High School for the bi-district championship, and they were always a big power—strong German kids who could really run the sweep. Their quarterback had been injured, so they weren't much of a passing threat. But could they ever run the ball!

We played this game at Southwest Texas State University Stadium in San Marcos, the city where Mom and Dad had lived when I was born, and it was a big event for us.

The game began, and it was a pretty close one. They'd run the ball, use up the clock, and finally score. Then we'd pass and score in just two or three plays. One play, I remember, was a little dump pass I threw to Darrell. He caught it, cut across the field and up the sidelines. He was running over by our bench and Dad was running down the sidelines with him, stride for stride. At the same time, a train was passing the stadium, so with all the noise it was exciting to watch.

We finally won that game by a score of 35-28. I threw for over three hundred yards, with three or four touchdown passes; so with all the press there, it was an exciting time for us.

The following week we were set to play Corpus Christi Calallen High, and they were always great. We knew that if we won that game, we would play the other New Braunfels high school, and they were favored to take the state championship.

We arrived and the game started, with Calallen scoring quickly, again and again. They were quite a bit bigger than us. Our linemen's average height was 5 feet 10 inches, and the average weight was 190 pounds; Calallen's linemen had an average height of 6 feet 6 inches and an average weight of 240 pounds. It was easy to see that we were in trouble. We just couldn't stop them, and by halftime they were ahead 28-21. We felt that the only way they could beat us was to hold our receivers, and although I don't like to have sour grapes about the referees, it seemed that they were biased toward the other team.

The second half was frustrating because we could tell that nothing was going our way. We ended up losing that game by a score of 55-28, and it was one of the down points of my life. Even though I threw for over four hundred yards, we just couldn't get into the end zone as we should have.

I will have to say that at the beginning of the year Herman, Dennis, and Darrell had a little difficulty learning their positions; so we'd come out of the huddle, and I'd have to take extra time to tell each of them what their assignments were on that particular play. I didn't want them messing up, so it was worth the effort. Because of this, we were always the last four out of the huddle and I'd be pointing to where they lined up, giving them last-minute instructions. I never did find out if this helped the defense, or if it just confused them. But it sure helped us, because once Herman, Dennis, and Darrell knew their routes they were very effective!

Even though these guys didn't seem to have a priority of learning their routes, they knew how to loosen up and have a good time. Our locker room atmosphere before practices was an illustration of this. We'd go in to suit up, and they would turn on their ghetto blaster and have a dance-off. They'd be ripping on each other and having quite a good time.

It wasn't your typical drill-sergeant type of locker

room, because Dad wasn't that kind of a coach. He believed that football should be fun, and that team spirit and unity were the important ingredients for a winning program. He also knew that we would settle down prior to the game, but that our daily practices could be preceded with our having some fun.

We finished my junior year at 12-1, and even though we would have liked to take state, still we had gone further than ever before, and the spirit on the team was great. I felt that I was able to make a contribution, both as quarterback and as a team leader. When the season finally ended, I was fortunate enough to be named to the second team all-state, and to win the MVP for the state of Texas.

Basketball season then began, and I made varsity. We got to the play-offs, too, even though we didn't have much height. But because of how short we were, we lost in the first round. I started as guard and probably averaged ten to twelve points a game, with my high game being around twenty-two or twenty-three points. We had a couple of other players on the team who could shoot and who were the team leaders—so it was a lot of fun.

MY FIRST DATE

Having a girlfriend during my younger years was never one of my goals. Like the other guys, I didn't like girls when I was little, although I did kind of like a girl named Debbie Smith when I was in the fourth grade. Still, other than riding my bicycle over by her house without her seeing me, I pretty much kept my feelings to myself. I was just the shy type, I guess.

Other than that and secretly liking the girl named Jenny in the fifth grade, I really didn't have much to do with girls. Even when I was a sophomore, I knew that I wouldn't ask anyone out anyway, so I didn't even have to think of whom I *might* ask! After games, we'd go to one of my friends' homes and stay over. We'd then play basketball the next morning, and things like that. But we never really did much with girls. Once in a while they'd show up at someone's house where we were, and we'd laugh and have fun. Still, there was never really initiative on our part to get together with them.

When I was a junior, however, I finally gained the courage to go on my first date. I was turning eighteen the last of October, so I figured it was about time to go out. There was one girl named Alicia Williams who had impressed me, and I figured that I could ask her to go out with a group of us the following week after the basketball game. I took four classes with Alicia, so I planned on asking her out after one of these classes.

Well, the classes came and went, and the days passed, but I kept getting chicken. Finally, at the end of the last class on the day of the game, I walked up to her as we were walking toward the door. Without thinking of how hard it was to do, I just blurted, "Would you like to go get something to eat after the game?" I'm sure she would have turned me down if she could have thought of an excuse. But she said yes, and that began a good friendship for both of us.

The difficult thing about getting a girlfriend was the pressure of attending the junior prom. There was really no way out of that obligation, so I finally asked Alicia to attend it with me. I then braced myself for my first tuxedo. Even though I enjoyed the evening, I didn't really like to dance, and wearing that tux throughout the evening was one of the hardest things I had ever done. We triple dated that night with a couple of my friends: Kevin Lyssy and his date, Dawn Casper, and John Bordano and his date, Page, whom he later married. Because my folks owned a Cadillac, I volunteered to drive. This was great, and driving that beautiful car made it more enjoyable.

FINISHING OUT THE YEAR

I really enjoyed baseball that season, as I was able to hit .567, pitch a few innings, play shortstop and second base–and make all-state.

I also ran track on varsity, again running just fast enough to make the finals in the hurdles. Actually, I hated track because I hated to *just* run. I was doing it to improve my speed for football, but still it was more of a job than an enjoyment. I guess when it came right down to it, I hated it because I knew I wasn't fast enough to come in first place. I would do all right in the trials, but when the eight men lined up for the finals, I would almost always finish last. I did get a break sometimes when somebody else would trip over a hurdle and fall, and then I'd only finish seventh. But always, it seemed, I would finish last, and that just wasn't my idea of having fun.

I've often thought of my need to win and of what has made me so competitive. Part of it was my dad, because to this day I have never beaten him in anything, except golfing and hunting. It was also my younger brother, Koy, because until he grew up I could pretty much beat him in anything I tried. But in the neighborhood and on my teams I developed an attitude of never settling for second place, and I guess this has become part of my personality. My goal wasn't really to beat someone else, but rather to just be the best I possibly could be. I've always thought it important, as well, to let my opponents know when they've made a good play, or when they've played a good game against us.

Another characteristic of running the hurdles was that during the race I would flat-out sprint the entire distance. I couldn't start out slow, because then I wouldn't be in contention. Instead, I would have to sprint right from the starting blocks. This was hard because by the time I came to the last hurdle, I would aim for it and then stumble across the finish line. I never could get enough oomph to clear that last hurdle. In fact, I found myself almost aiming for it on purpose so that I wouldn't have to jump higher.

I played golf again my junior year, still being the only other player on the team. Again I shot about a ninety in the tournament—just enough to let me enjoy the day out of school on the links.

GETTING A *REAL* DEER

When hunting season rolled around my junior year, I was excited to go out with Dad and Koy. This was the time in my life that I became serious about hunting deer, and I have to say that I wasn't disappointed in how things turned out.

My dad was invited to hunt on a private ranch down near a place called Bruni, Texas, and Koy and I were able to accompany him. This was Thanksgiving weekend, so after we had our turkey dinner the three of us headed out, all excited about bagging a big buck.

We pitched our tent by a windmill, had a little dinner, and then went to bed. We didn't like to use a blind, so we thought that the following morning we would just take our stools and sit at various points along the road, and then see what came across.

From what other hunters had told us, we knew where a big buck had crossed on his way to cover. It was probably twelve hundred yards between the two blinds, six hundred in each direction from where we stayed. That night Dad asked us where we wanted to hunt, giving us our first choice. Koy said that he wanted to stay close to camp because there were always deer around there. He was about twelve at the time, and I think that gave him a little security.

I said that I would hunt the back fence line, since the big buck had been seen crossing the fence before.

Morning came before we knew it, and soon we were each positioned on our stools, waiting for daylight to arrive. It got light about seven o'clock, and about an hour later I heard Koy shooting from where he was. I figured he had shot a doe, since he had a doe tag; or maybe a javelina, since he was pretty trigger-happy. As long as it moved, he would shoot at whatever was legal.

At that moment a wild hog came about ten yards from me, directly across the fence from where I was sitting. I was trying to decide whether to shoot that or to wait for a possible shot at a buck. But I knew that one buck might show up, so I held tight. Finally the hog saw me, and he took off into the trees.

A few minutes passed, and I was thinking about "Texas rules": we count the number of points on each side of a buck's antlers, add them up, and that number equals what we shoot. Up until this moment, the biggest buck I had bagged was an eight point, with four points on each side. I was in the eighth grade at the time, living in Laredo, and I thought quite highly of myself for getting it—even though it was limping along, wounded, when I finally dropped it. It was a good buck, too, but now I wanted to do better.

About an hour later, I saw some large, dark antlers coming through the fence. Usually when dark antlers become apparent, it means that it is an older deer with a pretty good rack. I knew this would be the biggest buck of my hunting career, if I could bring it down, so my heart was just pounding.

The buck was about ninety yards away from me at the time, and when he ducked under the fence, I clicked my safety off and aimed. He heard the click and lifted his head, warily looking in my direction. I knew then that he had a pretty good rack, and even though I couldn't see too clearly, I aimed behind the shoulder and fired.

He lunged forward, stumbling, so I shot again and

finished him off. I was shooting a .270 with a 3X9 Red-field scope that I had just gotten for my birthday, so I was psyched to be shooting it for the first time.

I then ran down to where the deer lay, and was I ever excited with its size! I hurried and gutted it out, then dragged it into the brush so I could surprise my dad.

I finally sat down, and about ten minutes later our green and white Scout pulled up. We had two dogs, a half Doberman, half Lab named Booger, and a good-sized Rhodesian Ridgeback named Moses. Moses was the same breed of dog that had been used over in Africa to hunt lions. So we used both Moses and Booger to trail the deer after we had shot them.

Anyway, Dad, Koy, and the two dogs came down the road about fifty yards from me. So I got up and dragged my buck out of the brush to show it off. I need to say that Dad had never killed a buck with a 20-inch rack before. He'd killed bucks with 19-inch and 19½-inch racks, but never one with a 20-inch rack.

Well, Dad was surprised when he got to me, since he had thought I killed a doe. His words said it all: "Ty, that might be a 20-inch spread!" But the longer he looked at it, the more convinced he became that it was even bigger than that. In his mind, the antler spread grew the longer he looked at them. He then said, "That's probably a 22-inch spread."

We loaded the buck on top of the Scout, and after hoisting it up, Dad got out his tape measure to see what I had bagged. We were surprised when he exclaimed, "Well, I'll be darned if it isn't a 25¾-inch spread! I can't believe it! And to think that I let you hunt here!"

All I could think at the time was that this was a true father speaking—one who had the hardest time not winning! Then he said something that I'll always remember: "Ty," he smiled, "I'm really happy you got it!" And he was, too. He always wanted us to experience the thrills, so he would push us to the front of things.

We then climbed into the Scout, and I asked, "Well, what did Koy shoot?"

"Oh," Dad answered casually, "he just got a doe."

Koy didn't say much of anything, but just kept silent. When we finally got to where his deer was, I looked behind the brush and there was an eleven-point buck! Mine was a ten-pointer, and his was one bigger! I looked hard and exclaimed, "Dang, Koy, you got a big deer!"

Koy's deer had more of a basket rack, while mine was spread out; but he sure was proud to have gotten a deer with one more point than mine. His rack measured nineteen inches across, and the tines were higher than mine, but I knew that when we turned the racks in for inspection, mine had a good chance of placing in the largest buck contest.

Koy then told me the story of how he had killed his deer. He had hit it in the hind flank, but it hadn't gone down. So he and Dad had taken off after it, using the dogs to track it down.

As a general statement about the dogs, Booger was the best trailer, so she would follow the blood trail whenever a deer was hit. Moses would just follow behind. When Booger would get to the dead deer, no matter where it was, she would just howl until we got there. Moses, on the other hand, would begin dragging the deer out to where we could see it. They were a good team that way. Booger would find them, and Moses would drag them.

But on this hunt, the dogs took off, and Dad could see the deer every few seconds, as it bounded through the thicket. He then saw the deer jump over a cactus at a pretty good clip, and he was surprised to see that Moses bounded in hot pursuit over the same cactus. Somehow, Moses and Booger had gotten their assignments mixed up.

Dad and Koy finally got over to the deer and took care of it, while Moses and Booger both sat there, panting all proud-like.

We took the two deer in right away to Freer, Texas, to be measured for the "Muy Grande Deer Contest." We didn't want them to lose weight, so we had to hurry.

My buck eventually won first place for the state of Texas, and was I ever proud! I won a .44 Magnum pistol, with a five-diamond, gold-plated stamp on the butt, and it turned out to be a really nice pistol. I let Dad keep it in his safe, just so he could feel that he was part of it, but he knows the gun's mine and that one day I'll lay claim to it.

OUR FAMILY'S TRIP TO PROVO AND BYU

When my junior year of school finally ended, I knew I had some big decisions to make regarding my future. I was being recruited by quite a few major universities, so I had made a list of my top ten choices. Brigham Young University was first because they were a pass-oriented football team, and because of the mountains and the beautiful country there. Neil Reed, our assistant basketball coach, let the Y know about me. He had been an assistant basketball coach at the University of Kentucky under Coach Adolph Rupp, and had coached men like Pat Riley, who himself was in the process of winning four NBA championships coaching the L.A. Lakers. So I had a lot of respect for Coach Reed.

The Cougar coaching staff had subsequently been in touch with my father regarding me. I was also being recruited by Miami, Washington, Michigan, Stanford, and a few other universities.

So we left Texas as a family and drove north to Utah, with BYU being our first stop on a swing that would allow me to consider my final choices. If they weren't too interested, we were going to swing down to UCLA, then over to Arizona State.

We arrived in Provo and checked into the Excelsior

Hotel. Coach Claude Bassett had been to Texas to watch
spring practice, so Dad knew who he was. As a result,
we made an appointment with him, and were soon sitting in his office on campus. He was the defensive linebacker coach and recruited Texas players, so he was acquainted with my dad as well as with my high school
playing experience.

I was pretty quiet during our visit. I just listened to
Coach Bassett as he told us about BYU. We then went to
meet Coach Edwards, and his secretary, Shirley, showed
us the way to his office. She seemed happy to greet us,
and our meeting began a special friendship. When we
entered Coach's office, he got up and introduced himself. This was the first time he and I had met, although I
had seen him being interviewed on TV before. And even
though I wasn't as large framed as he probably thought I
would be, he was still very cordial and treated our family
with respect and genuine care. He was pretty low-key
during our conversation, but made us feel that we would
be very welcome at the Y.

Later, during the morning session of his camp for
young football players, Coach Edwards indicated that although he was not able to sign a scholarship agreement
with me at this time, after I graduated the following year
he would have a full scholarship waiting for me.

Our family then went out to lunch, and I spent some
time thinking about what Coach Edwards had said, and
what I should do. I thought of how beautiful Utah was,
and how enjoyable it would be for me to be in a small-
town atmosphere. I also wanted to go to a college that
was away from the mentality of many I had grown up
around—where players were academically oriented and
not just consumed with some kind of sport, or with girlfriends and social status.

From the media exposure BYU's football team had
received when they won the NCAA championship, I had
grown up respecting BYU's program, and I knew it was

a class organization. In addition to these factors, we looked at the quarterback situation, and we felt that I would have a chance of eventually working into a starting role.

I also wanted to go into a good neighborhood environment where the people were kind to each other—just good people. That was important to me because it was the kind of person my folks had always taught me to be. Not to be better than others, but just to be *good*. I knew I wanted to be happy, and I honestly felt, as my parents and grandparents had taught me, that this happiness was gained by choosing to be a kind and good person.

In essence, although I knew the people at the Y weren't perfect, still it would be a good, clean environment that would help me become the kind of person I wanted to be.

Later that day, following the afternoon session of camp, we were again standing on the sidelines, watching the way Coach Edwards and his staff were working with the youth. When he saw us, he came over again to visit. At that time I told him that my decision had been made to attend the Y. He seemed happy about this decision, and told us that the school and the team would do all within their power to see that I received a complete education. He also assured my parents that even though the school was privately owned and operated by The Church of Jesus Christ of Latter-day Saints, there were many students attending who were of other faiths and that my religious beliefs would be respected. I think my folks appreciated Coach Edwards's sincerity and his straightforward approach, and we all felt good as we left the practice field.

We spent the next few days fishing in the Provo River, touring around town and up the canyons, and getting acquainted with the campus. We then said good-bye to the coaches and others we had met, and instead of visiting the other campuses, we drove directly back to Texas. My folks had given me the agency of making my own decision, I had done it, and we were all happy with it.

This early decision made it easier for me during my senior year, since I knew where I was going and didn't have to entertain the various recruiters from the colleges that had previously expressed an interest in me. I was able to concentrate on school and on enjoying my last year playing for my dad.

BACK IN TEXAS—MY SENIOR YEAR

I was quite pumped up for my senior year at Southwest, and felt that in addition to athletics, I could really enjoy my classes. Things went well for me, too, and I earned good enough grades to be inducted into the National Honors Society.

I had grown to a little over 6 feet in height, with a weight of about 160 pounds on a "Big Mac day." I had worked out hard that summer, played golf, and fished, so I was ready for school and football.

During my freshman and sophomore years I had worked at a convenience store and gas station, and had pumped diesel and propane—besides being a gopher—and I enjoyed the work. I had made $3.30 an hour, and had been quite content until I learned that one of the fellows I worked with was unstable and unpredictable in how he treated people. As a result, I quit the job, since my mom didn't want anything bad happening to me.

Since that time, I had concentrated on working out during the summers and playing hard, so I hadn't gotten another job. May dad felt that the winter school and sports were so demanding that I needed a little time to wind down. I was glad for his approach, too, because it really did help me get mentally ready to play each fall.

After football season, I did get one other job that didn't really set well with me. A guy called me and told me that he had seen me on TV, and that he thought because I had a good smile and clean looks, I could do well modeling clothes in magazines.

Even though I wasn't quite sure of this job opportunity, I agreed to meet this guy and have him take some pictures. I was basically interested in some quick money, and I figured that maybe this was my chance.

I went down to the mall, as agreed, and he took pictures of me in several different outfits. I would pose playing the arcades, and things like that. But I was getting tired of it after only five minutes. People were looking, and it just wasn't me.

Still, I felt obligated to the man, since I had told him I would do it. We then went out to a park so that he could get some shots on the football field. I was wearing shorts, and he had me sit on the bleachers and then said, "Okay, take off your shirt, and we'll get some shots of you without your shirt on." I silently but uncomfortably obeyed, and then he said, "Okay, now lean back and flex your muscles." Well, what he didn't know was that I already was flexing, only he just couldn't see it. "I *am* flexing," I exclaimed, "*believe* me!"

He wanted to meet with me again, but by this time a little spirit just kept warning me. So when I got home, I had my mom tell him that I just couldn't make it. I never did get paid because I never wanted to see the guy again—but I sure did learn to follow my feelings.

Football season finally began with two-a-days. But my good buddies had gotten into heavy drinking during the summer, so we had grown apart. Because of this, even though our team was ranked fourth in the state in the preseason polls, I was concerned about our true potential.

In addition to this lack of personal commitment among several of the players, during the final scrimmage before our first game, Herman tore up his knee and was out for the season. He was the spunk of the team, and when this happened something was not quite the same for us. It just wasn't as much fun.

Because of this adversity, we finished with seven wins and three losses, and didn't even make the play-offs. It wasn't as good a season as we had hoped for, but in retrospect it was probably better than it should have been.

In addition to the drinking, there was a spirit of self-ishness that entered the team. Most of the individual leaders wanted to get the ball, be written up in the press, and earn individual glory. But I knew from Dad that this would destroy the potential of a team, and I guess in the end this is about what happened.

We actually started out 0-2, and then we got better. But it was never like the year before.

I was pretty fortunate personally, since I broke the career passing record for the state of Texas. The previous record for 4-A competition was a little over 5,000 yards, and I had such quality receivers for those three years that I threw for 8,005 yards.

My best game statistically was actually the last game of the year. In this game I threw for over five hundred yards. So I was quite satisfied with my own growth as a quarterback, even though I felt that as a team we didn't play to our potential.

I was also happy, in spite of our record, to be named to the first team all-state, even though I didn't receive the MVP award that year. This sort of made up for our team's record, but I would have traded it to have been able to go into the play-offs again as we had the year before.

Basketball season then began, and because we had lost a couple of our starters, we didn't have as good a team. We finished the season as the third-place team in our district. I was able to score thirty-three points in one game, which was a career game for me, and I averaged eighteen points a game for the season. Mike Harris was our coach, and he was like my dad in that he wanted us to be loose and to have fun while we were applying ourselves. Coach Harris's greatest coaching quality was emphasizing team unity.

Our last game finally arrived, which was with Pleasanton. This was now to be the final basketball game of my career, and we were playing at home.

The game was a rough one, too, with a lot of physical contact. I received a pretty fat lip on one exchange, but that didn't really bother me. The thing that *did* bother me was that three of our players showed up intoxicated. When we were warming up, and while the coach wasn't on the court, one of these guys would get down on the floor on his hands and knees while another of them would jump on his back and slam dunk the ball.

I wanted us to look good for the last game, and seeing this behavior kind of ticked me off. One of my closest friends was one of these players, and that made it especially difficult for me. As I saw him mentally deteriorate because of his growing dependency on alcohol, I became even more firm in my resolve never to drink, myself. It destroyed him, just as it did many others I had grown up with.

We won the game, even though we probably shouldn't have, and although the season ended on an upbeat as far as our fans were concerned, I was personally very disappointed. I knew that we hadn't played up to our potential, either in football or basketball, so this took some of the satisfaction out of my senior year.

Baseball season then began, and this season I played center field, shortstop, and pitcher. I only batted about .350 that season, and as a team we won only five games. We just weren't that good, but I still enjoyed playing. We did have a good next to last game of the season as we beat our rivals, South San West Campus. We lost our final game, though, and this seemed to sum up our senior year for us.

The golf tournament came around again, and as before there were still just two of us on the team. The tournament was scheduled for one day a week, three weeks running, and we enjoyed competing in that. Dad was the coach of our team, so he and I enjoyed ourselves as I shot rounds of eighty-eight, ninety, and ninety-two for the three days.

I wish I could say that I improved in track, but again I ran the 330-meter intermediate hurdles. And, as in the previous years, I seemed to only be fast enough to make the finals. Then, as before, I would place last in the finals. I also ran the high hurdles that year, and as usual I barely made the finals in that event, as well.

In thinking of my high school athletic experience, I have to really give my dad credit. He was the one who thought I should gain experience in as many sports as possible. This allowed me to graduate with more than just a football mentality. Because football is such a big thing in Texas, some coaches wanted their players to specialize in just that sport from the time they were ten or eleven years old. But not my dad. He wanted me to live my life to its fullest, and I have always respected him for this. He also told Koy and me that we should play a sport until it's no longer fun—then we should do something else. I hope to pass the same philosophy on to my own children, as it keeps things in perspective.

HIGH SCHOOL GRADUATION

Graduation day finally arrived, and the commencement exercises were to be held inside for the first time in years. We had moved into a new school campus during my sophomore year, so they finally decided to use these facilities for an inside graduation ceremony.

About the time the graduation program began, the power went out, and I thought when it happened that the outage seemed to be typical of our entire senior year. Things just didn't go right.

But I did graduate—in the top ten, actually, so my folks were happy about this. Our graduation class consisted of about two hundred students, but only about half of these qualified for graduation.

After enjoying a few weeks of fishing and being with the family, we packed my belongings in preparation for my move to Utah. Finally, as we drove north on Interstate 10 toward Kerrville, en route to the Y, I knew my life was going to change from that day forth. No longer would I have the security of living with my family, but instead I would have to make my own decisions.

I didn't know what was in store for me in college, but I did know that whatever happened, I could take the things I had learned from my parents and grandparents—as well as from all those who taught me in any way—and that I could succeed if I applied those things I had learned. I believed in God and in Christ, and I knew that if I treated others as I had been taught, perhaps I could make a little difference in someone's life. College was going to be great!

To BYU and Destiny

My dad's parents, Maw Maw and Paw Paw, came to Provo with us, so we caravaned from Texas to Utah in two separate cars. We had a good trip, arriving in Provo the first week of July. We stayed in the Excelsior Hotel, then enjoyed the Fourth of July celebrations, including the parade and Alan Osmond's spectacular Stadium of Fire presentation.

MY FIRST VEHICLE

Because my folks wanted me to have a vehicle that I could depend on through the Utah winters, as well as use in hunting in the rugged Rocky Mountains, I bought a year-old 1986 Blazer Silverado shortly after we arrived in Utah. It was white with a gray underlining and had only ten thousand miles on it. I was quite pleased. I used my savings to buy part of it, and my grandparents gave me the money to completely pay it off so that I wouldn't have monthly payments to make.

My sister Dee also needed a car, since she was starting school at Missouri Valley College (because I had stayed back a year in junior high school, we both graduated from high school together). So she bought a Dodge Laser the day after I bought the Blazer. Our whole family was involved in the purchases, so it was quite an event. Dee then drove her car back to Texas with the others.

I'll never forget leaving the car dealership with my newly purchased four-wheel-drive Blazer. Koy, who was thirteen years old, was riding with me, as was Dee; and other than my telling Koy to keep his feet off the seat, we pretty much rode away in silence. We had to go to Coach Bassett's home to show him my new wheels, and even though we weren't saying anything, I was proud as can be—proud to be going to BYU, to be leaving home, and to be the owner of such a nice automobile.

A NEW FOOTBALL CAREER BEGINS

While my family was still in Utah, I moved into Helaman Halls—Chipman Hall, actually—for two-a-days, and then into Hinckley Hall once school began. Brian Mitchell, a Texan like me, was also starting out at the Y, as a defensive cornerback. So we had stopped in Waco and picked him up on our way to Provo. He then became my first college roommate, and we roomed together until fall, when I moved in with Dave Henderson, a strong safety, who was from Longview, Texas. Dave and I roomed together for the first semester, and have been best friends since that time.

About the same time I arrived in Provo, the returning players also came back, and we would throw the ball, work out with conditioning, and in general just get to know each other. The other quarterbacks—Bob Jensen, Sean Covey, and Mike Young—all worked with me so that I could begin learning the basics of how the team moved their offense. We worked with great receivers like Chuck Cutler, David Miles, Jeff Frandsen, Matt Bellini, and others, and it was a great feeling to be throwing the ball to such gifted athletes. Bob Jensen was the starting quarterback, so he was the unspoken leader, and he saw to it that I was accepted as one of them.

Still, there were some wrinkles to work out. One day we went to practice, and there were ten receivers and six quarterbacks, including Brent Smith, who was also a freshman like me. The final quarterback, other than those named above, was Ralph Martini. Anyway, since Brent and I were the freshmen, the other quarterbacks sent us over to the side of the field and said that there weren't enough receivers for all of us to throw to. I'll admit that this upset me quite a bit. I figured that I was on full scholarship and that I should be treated equally with the rest of the quarterbacks. Even though the coaches weren't there, because it was too early for them to begin formal practices, still I was upset. So Brent and I just worked with each other, without rotating. To put it mildly, that was not a very happy day for me.

I've thought a lot about that experience in the years since then, and whenever there haven't been enough receivers for all the quarterbacks, I've gone out and run receiver routes so that the others could throw. I'm not putting myself above the other quarterbacks, but I've always tried to treat the others as being equal with myself.

School finally started, and although I redshirted that first year, still I was the third-string quarterback. Mike Young had quit during two-a-days so that he could concentrate on his premed classes, and Ralph Martini was injured. So I was lucky enough to travel with the team, even though I was being redshirted. We went to Australia and Hawaii, too, which was quite a thrill for a young man from south Texas.

My only regret during that season was not having any more fun than I did. The coaches were always playing with my mind, telling me that I had to be ready to play, just in case I was needed. So I was pretty serious about things, and never did allow myself to loosen up and just enjoy life.

BYU lost to Pittsburgh, in Provo, the first game of the year. It was a night game, and ESPN was covering it. Having never played in front of a crowd of more than thirteen to fifteen thousand people, I was charged up. Even though I wasn't actually playing, I'll never forget the emotion of coming out of the tunnel while sixty thousand fans yelled at the top of their lungs. My hair stood up on the back of my neck, I was so excited. I realized at this moment that I was now involved in college football, and it was quite an exhilarating emotion.

When the Texas Christian University game arrived, we traveled to Ft. Worth, Texas, and had an experience with crickets that I'll never forget. They flew onto the field by the thousands, and I felt as if it were the crickets invading the Mormons all over again.

Bob Jensen, our quarterback, got hurt during the game, and he was replaced by Sean Covey. Sometime during the third quarter, I became quite impatient because we weren't throwing the ball up the field as I thought we should. So I went up to Coach Chris Pella and asked, "Coach, when is it my turn to play?" His reply was predictable, as he just said, "Stay ready, Ty. You never know when you'll be needed."

This was the first time I remember thinking that I could actually do the job of starting quarterback, and I didn't care that I was redshirting. But again I didn't play, although I felt emotionally ready for it.

MY FIRST UTAH DEER HUNT

Ever since my family and I had seen the mountains to the east of Provo, I longed for the moment when I could take my rifle and could bag my first mule deer. The deer in Texas were mostly whitetail and were much smaller.

But to stalk a big mulie was an experience I had always looked forward to. I had eaten many a venison steak prepared by my mom, and even though we enjoyed eating the harvested meat, the sport was something I really looked forward to.

I lived in the dorms, and because I didn't know where to hunt, I thought that maybe I should just go where I had been fishing—up South Fork in Provo Canyon, just a few miles from campus. Someone had told me that there were some big deer up there, although at the time I didn't know that he meant way up on top.

So I went with my friend Alan "Idaho" Michie, who, as his name clearly implied, was from Idaho. Like me, he had never hunted mule deer before, and so this was a new experience for both of us. I hadn't brought out my .270 rifle from Texas, because I didn't want to beat it up in the oak brush of Utah. Instead, I had brought out my grandfather's 30.06, which was a good rifle, and which had a nice 3X9 variable Redfield scope attached to it.

Anyway, early that morning we drove up the canyon, parked on the side of the road, and began hiking up from there. As I said, this was my first time to hunt in the mountains, and because I wasn't used to hiking a lot, I became tired very quickly. When it began to get light, I could see my car down on the road below us about two hundred yards away. Until that moment, I thought we had hiked forever. But then I realized that there weren't even any trees around us, and that we were still quite close to the road below us. We could see some deer that we thought were does across the canyon about a thousand yards away, as well as some more does about six hundred yards away in the other direction. But we never did see any bucks, and even though we went back up the other side of the mountain that afternoon, still we saw nothing, and so I wasn't even able to shoot my rifle.

I knew by this time that I wasn't the great white hunter I had made myself out to be. But then neither was "Idaho," so we were about even. Actually, I razzed "Idaho" for our getting skunked that day because he would kick the leaves and talk out loud, never seeming to understand the need to be quiet. This was exasperating, too, and I figured we weren't going to see anything, so we headed back to the car.

I knew there was always another year to hunt, but it sure was hard on my pride not to be able to call home and let my dad and Koy know about a big buck I had gotten. Little did I know at the time that I wouldn't get a buck the next two years out, either. Instead, I would learn patience and humility, and have to just settle for eating some good camp-fire meals and enjoying the majestic beauty of the fall Utah mountains.

BACK TO FOOTBALL

At the end of my redshirt season we played the University of Virginia in the All-American Bowl in Birmingham, Alabama. Although we were beaten by a touchdown, I had a nice trip into the Deep South, and I enjoyed the game from the sidelines.

MOVE FROM THE DORMS

I figured that one semester in the on-campus dorms was long enough for me, so when we returned from Christmas break, my friends and I moved into what was called "The Neighborhood." It was a four-bedroom duplex above Old Mill apartments in Provo. Dave Henderson came with me, and we moved in with Scott Charlton and Eric Mortensen. They wanted to get into a more residential environment, just as we did, so we moved into one side of this duplex at this time.

That spring Bob Jensen left to play ball in Canada,

so Sean Covey, a second-semester sophomore, became the starting quarterback for the spring game. He had actually replaced Bob as the starter during the last few games of the previous season.

When spring semester ended, I went back to Texas to be with my family. Again I spent my time working out each day, fishing, and just being with the people I loved.

MY PLAYING YEARS BEGIN

In the fall of 1988, I returned to the Y for my second year, even though it was my freshman year of eligibility. I was feeling good about school itself, and I felt more confident that this football season I had classes I could manage. The previous year, my first semester in college, Coach Bassett had loaded me up with some heavy classes such as Math 110, American Heritage 100, English 115, Psychology 111, and a couple of others. Although I didn't fail any of these classes, I barely passed, and had to really scramble to be eligible to play that fall.

But the school year began, and I was named second-string quarterback behind Sean Covey. By this time he was in his junior year of eligibility, and I was two years behind him. I felt good about my passing, and thought that I could come in as a backup and perform on the college level.

Our first game of the year was at Wyoming, and the game was shown nationally on ESPN. Sean was knocked out toward the end of the first half, and at last I had my chance to play. Sean had lost his short-term memory, and Coach Edwards told me that I would be playing the rest of the game.

On the first series that we had the ball in the second half, we drove down the field, and I threw a touchdown pass to Chuck Cutler. I thought it had been pretty easy; nothing to it, really—just like playing in high school.

That was when I learned a whole lot about humility, because in the next three series I threw three interceptions. Then I fumbled the ball on the next series. On the final series I again threw an interception, and we lost 24-14. That trip back to Utah was one of the longest of my life. I realized then that if I was going to play major college ball, I would have to turn my level of performance up a couple of notches. I had never seen such blitzing in my life, and I knew that I had to think more quickly if I was going to make a contribution to the team. The defense was bigger, faster, and more intelligent than I had previously seen, and I vowed that this would never happen to me again. In fact, looking back on it, I learned more from that game than any game I've played in— before or since.

The game with Wyoming was truly a baptism by fire. I knew that I wasn't as good as I had thought I was; but that game awakened me, too, and I knew that I had to learn from it. I also learned a lot about Coach Edwards, because after the game was over he came up to me, put his arm around me, and said, "Don't worry about it, Ty. Just keep your head up, and you'll do fine. No one has lost confidence in you. It was your first game, and you can use it as a learning experience." I was relieved that he hadn't come down on me, but instead had given me understanding and a continued vote of confidence.

Still, I wanted to make sure, for myself, that the team still had confidence in me, just in case I ever went back in. So I talked to the seniors and apologized for how I had played. I also told them that it would never happen again, but that they could count on me. Their response was positive; they expressed confidence in me and told me to just keep working hard. I felt pretty good after each of these conversations, and from then on I never looked back. I knew they were behind me, and if I was called on again I would perform to the expectations of myself, the coaches, and the team.

That weekend we played Texas in our first home game. We beat them quite badly, and so I went in at the end of the game and completed two out of three passes for sixty-four yards and a touchdown pass. It felt good, too, because the Austin papers had been writing that I was like a boy in a man's game, and that I was too small to play major college ball. They also said that my high school stats had been greatly overrated. So this had made me even that much more determined to succeed.

The next game was against UTEP, again in Provo, and we were behind when Sean was injured for the second time. Toward the end of the game I threw a touchdown pass to Freddie Whittingham, and we won by three or four points. It wasn't a flashy victory, but I felt I had played well, and so this was a big boost for my confidence.

MEETING A CERTAIN COUGARETTE

Following the Wyoming game at the beginning of the season, I received a nickname by a group of Cougarettes. I was not aware of it at the time, but among themselves they began to call me "Turnover." This nickname continued to spread across campus, and I was called "Cherry," "Lemon," "Apple," or whatever other turnover name they could come up with.

By the time my sophomore season began in the fall of 1989, that name had pretty much left me. But even before then, the girls who started it became my good friends. Two of these girls were the Herbert sisters, Misty and her older sister, Kim.

The first time I remember personally meeting Kim was at the conclusion of a date that she had with my roommate Scott Charlton. They came over to the house, and the rest of us were quite surprised because we had teased Scott about having a difficult time getting a date with a beautiful girl. But Kim *was* beautiful, and so we razzed him about that. He was pretty proud of her, though, so he wasn't bothered by it. Scott was really a good person, and so our teasing him was just our way of letting him know how much we enjoyed our friendship with him.

I'll let Kim tell about the next time we met:

"Actually, I met Ty for the second time just the next night. Before that, whenever I had seen him he had been with his high school girlfriend, Alicia. But this time when my roommates and I went over to his apartment on an unannounced visit, Ty wasn't with her or any other girl.

"I have to say that my impression of Ty to this point was that he was the shy, quiet type. He never said much, but just smiled and laughed with the others. He was *anything* but someone who wanted to be center stage.

"So my girlfriends and I were invited to sit down and play table games with him and his roommates. My sister Misty, our roommate Diana VanWagenen, and I were all there—and the more we played, the sillier we became. Before long, I began to notice how funny Ty was, and I remember thinking to myself, 'He's pretty cool.'

"We continued having fun, and before long Ty found a coat hanger and molded it around his head. He straightened out the curled part, and had it sticking straight out in front of him. He told us that this was his radar, his sixth sense, which allowed him to win whatever game he played. At the time I remember thinking what a crazy nut he was! But I've said enough, so he can take it from here."

At this time, Dave Henderson and I were not LDS. And so even though we considered ourselves good Christians, we decided to have some fun with these naive Mormon girls. Kim didn't know about my Methodist beliefs, and she asked me playfully, "What do you do, worship the sun or something?"

We picked up on that and announced that we were sun worshippers, and that the sun was our god. The amazing thing to us was how totally gullible these girls were, and how much they believed what we were telling them.

For the rest of this school year, we found ourselves having more and more fun with these roommates, in spite of how gullible they were. As "house against house," we would have all kinds of staged fights—usually with eggs and water and things like that.

ACADEMICS

That fall season was also quite fulfilling academically. I knew that the primary reason for my being in college was to receive an education, and even though I was enjoying myself both on and off the field, I was also gaining a deeper appreciation for my professors and for the things they were teaching me. I knew that learning didn't just take place in a classroom, but more and more I was thankful that my folks had stressed a college education. I felt good knowing that my mind and my view of life were growing and expanding. Someone once said that "knowledge in action is power at work," and I felt that with sports, as well as with life, I was gaining knowledge that would help me throughout my life.

I also found that as each semester rolled around, I had a greater capacity to perform and to earn the grades that I wanted. Even though football was consuming as much time as a full-time job, still I was able to hold my own academically and to steer away from any failing grades. Although I wasn't what you would call a bookworm, I *was* concerned about attending my classes and being responsible with the student scholarship the Y had given me.

FINISHING OUT THE FOOTBALL SEASON

Throughout the rest of our football schedule, whenever Sean got injured I would go in for a play or two. But it was usually on a second-and-twenty-five, or a third-and-eighteen, after he had been sacked, or some situation like that. So this wasn't especially fulfilling, since I didn't usually have the chance to perform without our backs being against the wall. But I enjoyed going onto the field whenever I got the chance, and the challenge of leading the team, even for just one play, was exhilarating.

Sean injured his knee prior to our playing New Mexico, so I was finally able to start a game. It was a good feeling to mentally prepare to start, something I hadn't done since high school, and I really felt ready to play when the game began.

My teammates rallied around me, too, and we had momentum and unity. Because of this, I was able to throw for over three hundred yards and complete five touchdown passes. That was a game—a win—that I'll always remember!

I didn't play at all in either the TCU or the Air Force games, but other than those I was able to get a little experience in each of the other games.

Still, the regular season ended with my having passed for about twelve hundred yards and thirteen touchdowns, and so for a freshman I felt pretty good about my contribution.

A FINAL "HOUSE AGAINST HOUSE" BATTLE

After the regular season ended, our "house" and Misty and Kim's "house" decided to have one final, all-out fun battle. None of us wanted to have to clean up our apartments, so we mutually decided to have this "war" outside, where we could just plaster each other.

When the evening arrived, Dave Henderson and I found ourselves set to battle with Kim, Misty, and Diana, three of the roommates we'd had fun with all that fall.

Dave and I decided to do it up right, so we went and caught some fish out of the Provo River. We put the fish entrails inside a bucket of water, and hid that in the bushes. Then we put cups of vinegar and cups of oil in different secret locations around the neighbors' yards. We hid eggs in places we figured they'd run to in order to escape, and before long we were ready.

The reason why we were so careful in our preparations was that earlier in the year they had come over and gotten us badly. They had used eggs, mustard, catchup, mayonnaise, tomatoes, and so forth. All of this had taken place in our "house," and even though we had gotten them pretty good at the time, still they had really worked our house over, so we were forced to spend quite a bit of time cleaning it up.

Anyway, it was now our turn, and even though we wouldn't go into their house, still we would ambush them outside *our* house, and really show who was the best.

After we had gotten all set up, the girls called us and told us their Cougarette practice had gone too long and that they wouldn't be able to make it. This really ticked us off, and we let them know that we thought they were chicken. Kim had wanted to participate in our big battle, but the others were trying to back out.

Our pretended anger changed their minds, and so before long they went out and bought a dozen eggs and came on over. They first drove by without stopping, and saw that there weren't any lights on in our apartment; they also saw Dave hiding in the bush. That made them pretty nervous, but they knew there was no retreat.

Before long they returned, and pretty soon we were in full battle. We used all of our arsenal, and Kim was so frustrated afterward that she climbed in our shower with her clothes on and clogged up the drain with all the ammunition that had covered her. She went home dripping wet, but she left all the mess in our bathroom.

The girls finally got back in their car and left, and even though the entire battle had ended quickly, still we had a great time. The girls always thought that the role

of "losers" in our battles went back and forth, with each
of us taking our turns at getting the worst of it. But we
guys knew, from our perspective, that it went more *forth*
than *back*. They were great sports, though, and so we
were happy to have them as our friends.

THE FREEDOM BOWL

By this time we were back in football practice,
preparing for our bowl game. We were excited because
we would be playing Eric Bieniemy of Colorado, and we
knew how good he was.

We played Colorado in the Freedom Bowl, down in
Anaheim, California, and that game was a crucial turning
point I'll never forget. By this time in the season there
was quite a bit of controversy about whether Sean or I
should be the starting quarterback, but I didn't want to
be part of it. I felt the team should be unified, and so
even though I would have liked to start, I did what I
could to be supportive of Sean.

Before the game began, Coach Edwards pulled me
aside and told me that Sean would be starting, but that if
things didn't go well I would play the second half. I accepted his decision and learned a real lesson at that time
about loyalty. I respected the fact that he treated Sean as
a person, as well as a skilled quarterback who had won
a lot of games for the Y. This gave me confidence in how
he would treat me in the future, when things might be
difficult for me.

From where I stood, Coach was walking a tightrope,
and he handled the situation better than most other
coaches would have. That taught me a lot about loyalty
and integrity, and I appreciate the private manner in
which he spoke to me.

I went into the game at the beginning of the second
half, and we were behind several points at the time. I

knew that I was mentally prepared to play, so I tried to think about my own job on the field.

We ran the ball pretty well throughout the second half, and I was able to throw for about 130 yards and one touchdown. We also penetrated twice after the touchdown and made two field goals that allowed us to come from behind and win.

We were all pretty happy after that victory, and I remember thinking as we flew home that I needed to compare myself *with myself* rather than with Sean. This concept really became part of my philosophy at this time, and has been good for me to remember as we have received the national recognition since then—with constant comparisons between my performance and that of other players from other schools.

My other thoughts at this time were of satisfaction in proving myself to the other players on our team. I felt this would be a good foundation for the following year, and beating such a fine team as Colorado, who would eventually win the national championship the following year, did a lot for our team confidence and expectations.

As summer began, we really felt that we would have a good shot at winning the WAC title, if we could apply what we had learned and then work hard to condition ourselves that summer.

This was also a difficult time for Sean in that he was forced to have knee surgery to correct the ligaments he had torn during the season. He knew this injury might limit his playing time during his final season; but he also knew that he had to be healthy if he was going to play at all, so the surgery was performed.

1989—MY SOPHOMORE YEAR OF ELIGIBILITY

After enjoying a few weeks again with my family

back in Texas, I returned to Provo and began to condition myself for what I hoped would be an even better year than the one before. A friend of ours, Rick Evans, who was on the wrestling team, wanted to live with us. But we didn't have five bedrooms, so Rick bought a home in Orem and we all moved in there and rented from him. He was a softie for a landlord, too, but he did expect the rent. So it was a good place for us to be. Because it was in a neighborhood, the neighbor kids would come over and play catch with us, and so this was great. Their mothers were also kind to us. They would make goodies and bring them over to us, so we felt pretty special.

Sean was recovering well from his knee operation, but was still not at a hundred percent. So when the second week of two-a-days began, I started taking the "reps" with the starters. The thing that made me feel good was that when the team captains were elected, the offensive players voted for me to be one of the two captains representing them. They also voted for Freddie Whittingham, so the two of us joined with the defensive captains in leading the team that season.

Even though I was happy with my own situation on the team, I knew Sean was having the same difficulties I would have had if our roles had been reversed. He came and talked with me; and from my point of view, this may have been Sean's finest hour. The coaches had told him that I would be the starting quarterback, with him coming in as my backup. So rather than quit the team, as he could have done, he came to me and told me that he would do whatever he could to support me in my starting role. For a senior to make this statement to a sophomore was impressive. The rest of the team knew this, too, and I think we were able to use Sean's example as a rallying point to work together to regain the WAC title.

Still, success would not come easily, as we were about to discover.

THE SEASON OPENER AGAINST NEW MEXICO

The season began with our playing New Mexico. By halftime we weren't doing well, and we were behind 3-0. We had moved the ball well, but we were beating ourselves with penalties and turnovers. So we hadn't gotten into the end zone.

But the second half we came out ready to play, and I was fortunate to be able to score our first touchdown on a bootleg. The Lobos were still in the game until Brian Mitchell scored on a ninety-seven-yard interception return at the end of the third quarter. This interception set a school record, and we knew there was no way they could come back on us. The final score was 24-3, and we were on our way.

GAME TWO—WASHINGTON STATE

We weren't as fortunate in the second game, however, as we lost to Washington State in the final minutes by a score of 46-41. I had done quite well, passing for 537 yards and four TD's; and Matt Bellini, Andy Boyce, and Chris Smith each tallied over one hundred yards in pass receptions. But even so, Washington was able to score on us, and so this left us at 1-1 for the young season.

PLAYING NAVY IN ANNAPOLIS, MARYLAND

Nine days later found us flying east of the Mississippi River for only the fourteenth time in Cougar football history. We were playing Navy, and we knew that they ran the option on offense, so we were pretty concerned.

Our concern was not unfounded, either, as they

scored on their first possession. But our defense got the hang of it, and the final score was BYU 31, Navy 10. The thing I remember about that game is that Navy had zero penalty yards, and I played the entire game without being sacked.

UTAH STATE IN LOGAN

The next week was a bye for us, and then we traveled north for our annual outing against the Aggies. We jumped out to a 14-0 lead, and won the game by a score of 37-10. Stacey Corley scored on runs for the first and last touchdowns of the game, but other than that, it was not a happy game. We were penalized fourteen times for 125 yards, and at one point the game was marred by a bench-clearing brawl which saw a player from each team ejected. I know that sometimes I get upset, just as most of us do. But I felt bad that we let tempers get the best of us. That situation has no place in competitive sports, and one of the great character-building moments in a person's life can occur if he will learn to control his temper under any such circumstance.

PLAYING THE WYOMING COWBOYS

Happy to be back in Cougar Stadium, our team played well as our next game, against Wyoming, began. We were of a mental set to avenge two previous losses to the defending WAC champions, and we jumped out to a 22-0 halftime lead. They bounced back with two third-quarter TD's, but our freshman wide receiver, Micah Matsuzaki, caught a twenty-nine-yard TD pass to put the game out of Wyoming's reach. We won by a score of 36-20, and even though this made us 2-0 in WAC play, the win was subdued by Rocky Biegel's having sustained a serious knee injury. We knew that would hurt us, and we hoped he could recover and be back soon.

THE COLORADO STATE GAME

We opened up a 19-0 lead in the game with Colorado State, but they came back before halftime and closed the gap to 19-10. Their coach, Earle Bruce, wore the suit Coach Edwards had bought him two years earlier in Provo, but this time we beat an Earle Bruce team for the first time in five meetings. Our kicker, Jason Chaffetz, had a big day on his native soil, booting four field goals and three PAT's.

UTEP IN PROVO

Back-to-back second-quarter interceptions returned for touchdowns by linebacker Bob Davis and safety Norm Dixon turned the game with UTEP in our favor. Another play that sealed their fate was a third-quarter fifty-four-yard touchdown pass to Stacey Corley. I felt good because in our winning 49-24 I had been able to throw to twelve different receivers. I tallied twenty-two completions out of twenty-eight attempts for 426 yards and three touchdowns, and was also able to score one rushing touchdown. It was a good game, and we were ranked eighteenth in both of the national polls.

HAWAII—A NIGHTMARE COME TRUE

We knew the game with Hawaii would be a hard-fought game, but what we didn't know was how fast we would be out of it. They came out with a no-huddle offense and were flawless, scoring on their first three possessions. Before we knew it, we were down 21-0, with the worst yet to come. Their quarterback, Garrett Gabriel, was nearly perfect in executing their run-and-shoot offense, getting 440 yards passing. While we had 427 yards passing, we were held to fifty-five yards rushing. Their defense sacked me ten times, which I could hardly believe—four of these by Mark Odom. This loss was hard to take, with the final score being 56-14 in their favor. We were now 6-2 overall, and 4-1 in the WAC. But still we weren't out of the hunt for the title, and so we flew back to the mainland with a renewed determination to do better. After all, we couldn't have done worse.

OREGON—IN PROVO

We did do better, too, defeating Oregon the next week, 45-41. It was a wild game, and they were ahead 33-14 midway through the third quarter. But Tony Crutchfield woke up the crowd and our team with a sixty-yard kickoff return for a touchdown. We then scored twenty-four points during a fifteen-minute stretch to take the lead 38-33. The Ducks went ahead 41-38, with three minutes remaining, but that just got us fired up. We went ninety yards in the next two minutes, and pulled out the win.

A CRAZY GAME WITH AIR FORCE

In the contest with Air Force, for the first time in six years Coach Edwards decided to receive the ball to begin the game instead of deferring. It paid off, too, when Stacey Corley returned the opening kickoff ninety-nine yards for a touchdown. We started celebrating too early, however, as they went ahead 17-7. But that was when Stacey returned a second kickoff, this time for eighty-five yards and a TD. It was a seesaw battle, with Brent Musburger and Kenny Stabler calling the action for a national CBS audience. We had the largest crowd in BYU history, but it might have cost us: six different times Dee Dowis, their quarterback, backed off the ball, saying that his team couldn't hear him because of the loudness of the crowd.

The game was still in question until Chris Smith caught a pass and broke several tackles in going forty-five yards for a score. We won the game 44-35, and not only did this keep us in first place in the WAC, but it made us only the third team in NCAA history to win one hundred victories in a decade.

GUNNING FOR THE UTES IN PROVO

With a desire to regain our respect, remembering Utah's win against us the year before, we came out smokin' when we played the Utes in Provo. Unfortunately their quarterback, Scott Mitchell, was out with a knee injury; we would have liked to beat them with him playing. But we went on a scoring rampage, and led 49-0 by the end of the first half. In that game I managed to move us down for touchdowns in all eight of the drives I participated in. My passing efficiency rating was 278.5, which was the best I had ever done; and Jason Chaffetz set a school record with ten PAT's in a single game, and at that point also broke the school record for consecutive PAT's with a total of thirty-six. It was a great game for us, and we won by a score of 70-31.

FINISHING THE SEASON AGAINST SAN DIEGO STATE

In the final game of the regular season, we rebounded from being down 14-7 to take a 35-14 halftime lead over

San Diego State. Although we shared the WAC title in 1985 with Air Force, this was the first outright WAC championship we had won since winning the national title in 1984. Our final record was 10-2, and we finished out the season ranked fifteenth and nineteenth in the two national polls. It felt great to regain the WAC championship, and I felt that the following year would be even better.

But for now it was back to the classroom and final exams.

WAC CHAMPS AND BACK TO THE HOLIDAY BOWL

The month of December went well, and before we knew it we were back in our pads, preparing for our bowl game. We had recaptured the WAC title, and so we were happy to be playing Penn State in the Holiday Bowl. Personally, I had played quite well that year, and had thrown for about 4,500 yards. Playing Penn State was a thrill for all of us because of Joe Paterno's great coaching history. They had a great team, especially defensively, but even so we were able to play well enough for me to pass for about 575 yards.

We had the ball toward the end and were driving downfield, with the score 43-39 in their favor. Even though we thought we were going to win, I had the ball literally stripped away from me by one of their defensive players when I was scrambling to pass, and he ran the other way for a touchdown. That was a pretty hard moment for me, because up until then we felt we could win the game. But they made the big play when they had to, so they won the Holiday Bowl by a score of 50-39.

It was a difficult loss for our team, but in a way, our offensive showing actually set things up for me to go through the summer as the leading candidate for the prestigious Heisman Memorial Trophy. Coach Paterno of Penn State may have done me more good than anything. After the game, he said that even though they had beaten the best teams in the country—including Miami with Testaverde, who threw five interceptions against their defense—they had never had a team do what we did to their defense.

We knew we had gained national respect as a contender, and even though we shied away from reading our own press clippings, we felt that our hard work and never-give-up attitude allowed us to look forward to the next season and what it might bring.

The announcement of the Heisman award was one of the most exciting moments of my career. What I didn't realize then was that my life would never be the same again. *(Photo by Mark A. Philbrick/BYU)*

My first football jersey.

Mom and I enjoyed watching Dad play for the San Antonio Toros, a semi-professional football team.

I began my football career on a flag football team in the first grade. By the time this photo was taken, I had graduated to tackle football and was playing quarterback.

My brother, Koy (right), and sisters, Dee (center) and Lori (left), have always been a big part of my life.

Playing several different sports in high school helped to keep things in perspective.

With my dad's encouragement, I was able to letter three times each in football, basketball, baseball, and golf at Southwest High.

I'll never forget this 1985 deer hunt with my dad and Koy. My buck won first place for the state of Texas in the "Muy Grande Deer Contest."

My first successful mule deer hunt was on this trip with BYU trainer George Curtis (at right with children), my cousin Freddie Buchholz (center), and special friend Kim Herbert (left).

It felt good to play, but I learned a lot about humility during my freshman year of eligibility. *(Photo by Mark A. Philbrick/BYU)*

I think one of the greatest discoveries a person can make is learning to find "balance." *(Photo by Mark A. Philbrick/BYU)*

Coach Edwards and I on the way to the locker room after a BYU home game. *(Photo by Mark A. Philbrick/BYU)*

Maw Maw and Paw Paw were thrilled with the announcement of the Heisman award.

My mother and two sisters met Kim and me in New York for the formal presentation of the Heisman Trophy.

I love football—not only for the high of winning, but more important for the experience of playing. *(Photo by Mark A. Philbrick/BYU)*

My philosophy has always been to live life to its fullest—to give each game my all. *(Photo by Mark A. Philbrick/BYU)*

A fan once told me, "You started with an interception, and you finished with an interception—but we liked everything in between." *(Photo by Mark A. Philbrick/BYU)*

I feel that our team's tradition of having a competitive spirit is important to personal growth and development. *(Photo by Mark A. Philbrick/BYU)*

Kim and I stopped to have this picture taken on our way to announce our engagement to her parents. (Photo by Russell D. Robison)

Our wedding announcement. (Photo by Russell D. Robison)

Kim and I on our wedding day. (Photo by Russell D. Robison)

My parents and many other family members traveled from Texas to be with us for the wedding. (Photo by Russell D. Robison)

Our "sort of" honeymoon in Hawaii.

Coach Edwards gave us advice on how to get four thousand people through the reception line. (Photo by Russell D. Robison)

Interviews with the press became a
regular part of pre- and post-game
activities. *(Photo by Mark A.
Philbrick/BYU)*

Kim and I had fun posing for this
Indiana Jones look-alike poster.

Receiving the Deseret News 1990 Athlete of the Year award from President
Thomas S. Monson (far right) with Kim's parents, Frank and InaLee Herbert.

I never thought anyone would ask for my autograph. (Photo by Mark A. Philbrick/BYU)

Mom has always been one of my biggest fans. (Photo by Mark A. Philbrick/BYU)

Mickey and Minnie were on hand for the Pigskin Classic festivities at Disneyland. (Photo by Mark A. Philbrick/BYU)

Saying good-bye after my final home game as a BYU Cougar. (Photo by
Mark A. Philbrick/BYU)

February 7, 1992—another beginning for Kim and me.
(Photo by Russell D. Robison)

Challenges, Growth, and Change

A SUMMER TO REMEMBER

When finals were over, I was really excited to spend a little time with my family, to unwind, and to mentally relax from all the pressures of school and football. I knew that I would only have a few weeks in Texas, since I had to return to Provo to work out and prepare for my junior season, so Koy and I made the most of it by fishing and doing things together.

Finally, about the middle of June, I said good-bye to my grandparents and headed back to Utah, knowing my family would be coming on vacation in a couple of weeks. When I arrived back in Orem, in a strange way I felt that I was home again, and I was happy to be there.

My family were to be in Provo for the Fourth of July Freedom Festival, to ride in Jack Sayers's antique automobile in the parade. I was also scheduled to be in the Pleasant Grove Strawberry Days parade a few days later.

I was glad to be back with my friends and fellow team members, not only to work out and prepare for the coming football season, but to enjoy those who were just friends, with no connection to football.

Among these friends was Kim Herbert. I had dated
her younger sister Misty a year earlier, and had even
gone with her to the Cougarette formal dance, but Misty
was working in Salt Lake City for the summer, and so
Kim and I basically had only each other to spend time
with. I really loved the Herbert family—and their kindness and friendship. In a way, I thought of Mr. and Mrs.
Herbert as my second parents, even then. Mr. Herbert
would tease me a lot, even though I would never let him
get the best of me. And Mrs. Herbert was kind and loving, like my mom, and this made it easy to be in their
home. I also appreciated the respect they had for me as a
person. They never pushed the Latter-day Saint faith
onto me, but were good examples, and let it go at that.

Kim and I didn't date, but we were friends—and by
the end of the summer we would become *best* friends. I
found out that summer that one of the jobs of being a
best friend is to give counsel and advice about whom the
friend is dating. And so even though I didn't go out with
anyone that summer, I *was* able to talk with Kim and
give her advice about whom she had a date with. We
laughed about that a lot, but we really enjoyed just being
with each other.

In fact, I have to share one experience that had taken
place the previous year when I thought up a scheme that
involved a make-believe date.

That night I called Kim up on the phone and told her
that I had a date with a really cute girl. I described the
girl's dark, short hair, even though she was only imagi-
nary, and Kim took what I was saying hook, line, and
sinker.

We talked on the phone for what seemed like forever,
with Kim telling me how to do this and that, and what to
do and not to do. I even asked Kim if I should kiss this
girl when I took her home, even though I would never
kiss a girl on a first date. She got pretty upset with me
and said, "No, Ty! You *never* kiss a girl on the first

date!" I laughed to myself, and just continued asking her questions, even though I really didn't have a *real* date. It was one of my more creative conversations.

Finally Kim wished me good luck on my date, I thanked her for her helpful suggestions, and our conversation ended. The next night I was gone for a while, as if I had gone on a date. I then came home and got ready for the next part of my joke on Kim and her roommates. I had told her that I was going out for a while, but that I was going to bring my date back to the house for a swim in our hot tub. She was pretty upset about that because she didn't think that was a proper thing for me to do.

Anyway, Kim and her roommates were pretty nosy and just couldn't keep away. I knew this would be the case, and so I climbed into the hot tub with "Idaho," and he positioned himself with the back of his head in the direction of where Kim and her roommates would look from inside the house—if they were brave enough to come over. We then pretended to be sort of making out, and sure enough, Kim and the others were peering out of the window toward the hot tub.

Kim takes it from here, as she recalls her reaction this way: "I was really upset to think that Ty, who was one of my very best friends, would actually be doing that on a first date! I just stood there and fumed! We headed back down to the car then, and Ty's other roommate, Dave Henderson, tried to coax us into coming back up. He finally succeeded, and when we got back there, Ty and 'Idaho' were just climbing out of the hot tub, laughing their heads off. It's pretty funny looking back on it, but at the time I couldn't have been more upset."

THE 1990 SEASON—MY JUNIOR YEAR

By the time two-a-days began, I felt that I was in good shape, and even though I hadn't gained much

weight during the summer, I was looking forward to what
the season would bring. What I was finding hard to get
used to was all of the media attention surrounding the
Heisman. Marion Dunn wrote for *The Sporting News
1990 College Football Yearbook:*

> Brigham Young quarterback Ty Detmer may not real-
> ize it, but he's about to become one famous young man.
> And yet all he cares about right now is UTEP.
>
> Detmer, whom former CBS sportscaster Brent Mus-
> burger called "the best-kept secret in America" last No-
> vember, won't be a secret much longer.
>
> Detmer now ranks as the quarterback with the best
> shot at this year's Heisman. And he'll get a chance to gar-
> ner some early votes when BYU hosts defending national
> champion Miami on September 8, in a game scheduled for
> national TV.
>
> So what weighs foremost on the mind of this junior
> quarterback? The dreaded Miners of Texas-El Paso, a
> team that won all of two games a year ago.
>
> "It will be something extra special to play a team like
> Miami here in Provo next fall, but I'm not thinking about
> that game right now," Detmer said last spring. "It will be
> Miami's opener, but it will be our second game. We open
> at UTEP, and that's a conference game. Our goal every
> year is to win the WAC and go to the Holiday Bowl. To
> win the WAC, we have to beat UTEP. So we have to think
> about UTEP before we start thinking about Miami."
>
> And he'll be thinking about the Hurricanes before he
> thinks about the Cougars' third opponent, and so on down
> the line. It's an attitude that endears Detmer to BYU
> Coach LaVell Edwards.
>
> "If there's such a thing as a coach's dream," Edwards
> said, "Ty's it."
>
> So when it comes to talk about the 1990 Heisman,
> nothing could be further from Detmer's mind. "I don't
> even think about that," he said. "I've still got a lot to
> learn, and I just want to improve each year."
>
> Edwards believes his quarterback's apparent indiffer-

ence to awards is genuine. "I don't think he's hung up on the Heisman Trophy," the coach said. "Ty just prepares to win. He realizes that winning will bring the awards. Awards are an outgrowth of success for Ty."

I appreciated what Coach Edwards said, because my goals have always been to improve my own level of performance and let the other things happen as they may. I just wanted us to have a good season and to play to our potential, and I knew the UTEP game would be a good test for us as we began the season, with this being our goal.

September 1 finally arrived, and we found ourselves warming up to play in the Sun Bowl in El Paso, Texas. By midway in the second quarter, however, things weren't going too well for us. We were trailing UTEP 10-7, and our players seemed to be distracted by the important game with Miami coming up the following week.

We finally settled down, though, and won by a score of 30-10. Coach Edwards expressed our sentiments best when, after the game, he said, "I think our defense is headed in the right direction. It was a typical opening night with lots of mistakes, but I'm satisfied with the victory."

THE GAME OF A LIFETIME— PLAYING NUMBER-ONE MIAMI

We returned to Provo relieved to have the first game out of the way, and to finally focus on playing the nationally top-ranked Miami Hurricanes. In a way, we knew this was the moment in the season when we could really show the nation what we were capable of doing on the football field, so we were psyched.

Allan Malamud, in writing for the *Los Angeles Times*, said it best when he wrote:

The Mormons like to tell this one on themselves. "How do you recognize a Latter-day Saints Church?" "It's the one with the satellite dish outside."

Such equipment is necessary because the networks still haven't discovered the Brigham Young University Cougars, who a while ago made college football the second most popular religion in Utah.

Winners of 102 games in the last decade, and the national championship in 1984, BYU will get a national cable audience only once this season—Sept. 8 against Miami on ESPN—and will appear on a regional basis twice. . . . Otherwise, tune in KBYU-TV, the campus station, if you've got a dish.

What a pity, because in the year of the quarterback, BYU may have the best.

I appreciated that Mr. Malamud put in the media my own feelings about playing for the Y, as I was quoted as saying: "You can be more focused on football at BYU than at other places. Besides, I never smoked, drank, or took drugs at home, so there's nothing different about that here."

Needless to say, not too many people around the country gave us a chance to beat Miami. Kurt Kragthorpe, however, of the *Salt Lake Tribune*, did make a positive statement by titling his pre-Miami article: "Y Faces Opportunity to Build Grid Legacy." We knew that there was a lot at stake with the Miami game, and that week was pretty intense as we made our preparations. The one thing I knew was that if we played to our potential, and didn't make costly mistakes, we would be able to win. It was exciting to even think about.

The game was not without its buildup, either. Miami players made comments to the press that were negative, saying that we were not always "clean-cut" players, and things like that. They said things about me, personally, which also rankled us. One of their star defensive backs said, "I want him to prove how good he is." Another one said, "Detmer's pretty good, but he's a long way from being great—a long way."

These and other comments continued to fuel our desire to win, and so by Friday night's team meeting, we were ready! I told Mark Smith to go into the meeting and fire everyone up and really get them going. No one had done that the previous week against UTEP, and I knew we needed that kind of intensity.

So in the meeting Mark got up in front of us, and tears got in his eyes right away. He was the perfect one for the job, and before long we were yelling and screaming about how we were going to pull the upset.

The next day, when we were warming up and receiving our last-minute instructions, the intensity was even higher than the night before, and I felt good about our mental preparation.

Coming out of the tunnel before the kickoff was even more exciting than the first time I had done it three years earlier. It was an evening game, and although I saw that the stands were packed even before the kickoff, I didn't learn until later that there was a stadium record of 66,235 fans attending the game.

The game finally began, and Miami's Stephen McGuire scored first on a seven-yard run. We then drove down and I threw a fourteen-yard touchdown pass to Matt Bellini to tie the score at 7-7. We drove the ball again, and Kauffman kicked a thirty-two-yard field goal midway through the second quarter. We then led 10-7.

After holding Miami again, we turned the ball over, and Miami's McGuire scored again, this time on a two-yard run. This meant they were ahead 14-10 with 1:42 left in the first half. I got pretty serious about then, and connected on seven straight passes, with the final one being a touchdown pass to Andy Boyce. The first half then ended, and we went into the locker room with a 17-14 lead.

We were all pretty excited in the locker room, and we

were given instructions on keeping our intensity up, but I don't think we needed to be told that. We couldn't wait to get back on the field and prove that the first half wasn't a fluke.

The second half began, and before we knew it their quarterback, Craig Erickson, had led his team on an eighty-yard drive that was capped by a Leonard Conley seven-yard run for the touchdown. They then led 21-17. We didn't know it then, of course, but those were the last points Miami would get.

We narrowed the gap a few minutes later on a twenty-nine-yard Kauffman field goal. This was with 9:26 remaining in the third quarter. A minute and a half later Miami made the error that may have cost them the game. They had the ball on a fourth-and-one, and instead of punting it they elected to go for it. What they didn't know was how good Rich Kaufusi was. He stopped McGuire for no gain, and we had possession of the ball. From there we went on a forty-three-yard drive that ended with a seven-yard touchdown pass to Mike Salido. I then threw a two-point conversion on a pass to Boyce, and we led 28-21. We stopped them two more times before the game was over, but finally the gun went off and we knew we had just beaten the number-one-ranked team in the country! We had earned twenty-seven first downs to their twenty-one, and felt that even though they were a great team, still we had beaten them fair and square.

I think the difference in the game was the fans. I told that to the press after the game, and they quoted me as saying, "Our fans were great tonight. They were on their feet the whole night. The student section right behind us really kept us going." Equally exciting was the fan response after the game. About two thousand of them ran onto the field, surrounding us and yelling at the top of their lungs. And the other sixty-four thousand fans just stood in their seats, screaming and whistling. Nobody wanted to leave, including the players. It was honestly one of the most exciting moments of my life.

The rest of the guys went out and partied after we had showered and left the locker room. But I was totally exhausted, both physically and mentally, and so I just went to our home in Orem and crashed. It was the biggest treat I could have given myself.

The newspapers across the country picked up on the game because of its national ESPN exposure, and they were very complimentary of our offense *and* defense. Rick Warner of the Associated Press said at the beginning of his article in the *Los Angeles Times*:

> Little Ty Detmer led Brigham Young to a huge upset over top-ranked Miami Saturday night.
>
> Detmer passed for 406 yards and three touchdowns as the 16th-ranked Cougars shocked the defending national champions, 28-21—only the Hurricanes' third loss in their last 55 regular-season games.
>
> "Ty Detmer is unbelievable," Miami Coach Dennis Erickson said. "He's a great, great quarterback and he showed it tonight."
>
> Detmer, who led the nation in passing last season, out-dueled Miami quarterback Craig Erickson in what was billed as a battle of Heisman Trophy favorites.
>
> "I don't think this one game will mean I'll win the Heisman," Detmer said. "I'm just glad I played well enough for us to win. I don't know what I do out there," said Detmer, who needed six stitches at halftime to close a deep cut on his chin caused by a Miami tackle. "I just run around and jump out of the way when I feel something coming. I guess I learned it from playing in the front yard."

I didn't like being called *little* Ty Detmer, but I had been told all my life that I was too little to play, and so it wasn't really anything new. What I did appreciate in that article, and the others that were sent to us, was that BYU was at last recognized as a national contender.

We vaulted up to number five in the rankings the following week, and we knew that we would no longer be a secret. Coach Edwards was interviewed, and he said: "The guys are really excited. But like I told them after the game, there's good news and there's bad news. The good news is that we just beat Miami. The bad news is that it's only the second game of the season."

We were playing Washington State the following week, and because they lost in an upset to Wyoming the day we beat Miami, we knew our hands would be full. We weren't wrong, either, because they led 29-7 by halftime. We just couldn't seem to put it together. We did score on a pass to Nati Valdez to open the third quarter, but were still behind 29-14 going into the final period.

Kurt Kragthorpe, the *Salt Lake Tribune* sportswriter, described what happened next in his article of the following morning. The article was titled: "4th-Quarter Explosion Fuels Y Win—Detmer Ignites 36-Point Burst":

> The interviews started last Sunday morning, hours after the upset of Miami. Day after day, BYU quarterback Ty Detmer was handling more requests, while this week's *Sports Illustrated* gave him a cover headline and a CBS-TV camera followed him around campus. "Kind of hectic week," Detmer would say later.
>
> Just another week in Ty-Land, really. Between questions and answers, Detmer found time for five touchdown passes in a 50-36 defeat of Washington State at Cougar Stadium Saturday afternoon.
>
> Down by 22 points at halftime and tied late in the game, Detmer kept firing. Last November's comeback from 19 points behind in the third quarter against Oregon is considered the vintage Detmer game, and the latest rally added to the legend: 36 fourth-quarter points.
>
> The final numbers: 32 of 50 passing for 448 yards, with two interceptions. So the Heisman Trophy campaign and the national-championship dreams live for another week, although you'll never hear that from coach LaVell

Edwards. After the game, Edwards told his players to stop talking about all that stuff, among other harsh instructions. "It's too early," Edwards told reporters later, sounding almost bitter.

I couldn't really blame Coach Edwards for feeling this way, either, because the media wouldn't let us rest for even a day. I knew he wasn't bitter, but was just concerned with such a steady distraction. It was a heavy price to pay, for all of us, but I felt that for my part I represented the rest of the team, and so I would keep my end of the bargain and accommodate them whenever I could.

The following week was even better for us, as we beat San Diego State 62-24. It was a nationally televised game by CBS, and I was fortunate to be able to throw for 514 yards, to give us a 4-0 start on the season.

THE OREGON GAME—A LESSON IN HUMILITY

The following week was pretty difficult for me in that I had missed practice all week. This was due to a ligament sprain in my throwing hand, and it was pretty tender. I couldn't grip the ball very well, but we didn't want the Oregon team to focus in on that and batter me when we played them, so we didn't tell anyone about the ligament problem until after the game. We made no excuses for it, but still it was quite painful to throw the ball— painful to even grip it, for that matter.

But we worked hard in the game, even though Oregon jumped out to a quick 12-0 lead. Their quarterback, Bill Musgrave, was one of the best, and he really had a good day. When it was over, even though we had out-passed their team 442 yards to 286 yards, they beat us by a score of 32-16. The game was telecast by ABC Sports, with Brent Musburger and Dick Vermeil calling the action, so we felt bad that we hadn't done well enough to win.

But this loss was a non-conference game, thank goodness, and even though it dropped us down to ninth and tenth in the polls, we were still confident that we could regroup and win the WAC.

The following week was our first bye week, and so we used it to get prepared physically and mentally for the rest of the season. I think we took out our feelings two weeks after the Oregon game, too, as we beat Colorado State 52-9.

A NEW BEGINNING

When I decided on playing at the Y, my high school girlfriend, Alicia, decided to move to Provo also and go to school there. We dated during our freshman year. But then as we grew older and became more of who we really are, we could see that there wasn't really a future for us together.

After my freshman year, I dated a few other girls for the next several semesters, mostly as lineups. I wasn't the most outgoing, social man on campus, and so I wasn't really aggressive in dating too much on my own. Even though I didn't go out too much, my roommates *did* go out and do a lot of "stylin' and profilin'."

I was now in my fourth year of college, and after having had such a great summer with Kim, I was really looking forward to getting to know her on a different basis. As the fall semester progressed, my friendship with Kim grew. Even though I was dating other girls, I felt that my feelings for Kim were deeper, and so we spent more and more time together. We were very respectful of each other's religions, and I went to her ward meetings whenever it was convenient to do so. She also attended church with me a couple of times. Because there was no Methodist church in the Provo area, we attended the Church of Christ, which met down on University Avenue. So she was willing to show her respect for me and for my beliefs, while continuing to share her testimony of the gospel every chance she got.

Late in September, after deciding that I wanted to check out my feelings for Kim, I called her roommate Diana and asked her if she thought Kim would go out with me. I didn't want to ruin the special friendship Kim and I had, so I had been afraid to just call Kim directly. But Diana assured me that I *should* ask Kim out, and from there it was only a matter of finding a time to be with her.

After I talked with Diana, Kim and I spent the evening walking around the streets of Provo—talking about everything under the sun. It wasn't a date really, but rather a time when we could sort out our feelings, and see if there was anything for us together in the future. It was a strange feeling, for both of us, but I also felt very comfortable being with her, so I was encouraged by that first evening together.

One of the things we talked about was my feelings that I should go to Salt Lake City to visit with her family and ask permission to date her. Because I had dated Kim's sister Misty the year before, and because I was so close to the Herberts as friends, I didn't want to do anything that would upset that friendship.

Well, Kim didn't think I would ask her out after that, but I was pretty excited about doing just that. Even though Kim doesn't remember my saying it, I told her that night that she was free to date whomever she wanted, even though I was going to date only her (subject to her parents' approval). My feelings were pretty strong, and I knew that if I was going to test these feelings, I needed to make that kind of a commitment to her. I never had enjoyed dating just to date, so this was a pretty serious step for me to take.

We didn't hold hands, or anything like that, through-out the evening. But when I went to say good-bye, I put my arm around her and gave her a hug to kind of let her know how I felt. We both went back to our apartments feeling good.

Kim remembers our first serious conversation, before we dated, as follows:

"I knew that if Ty and I were going to date, it would have to be on a more serious level than just to have fun. All my life I had been taught to prepare for an eternal mar-riage and to be true to the testimony of the restored gospel that I had acquired—so this had to be a consideration.

"Ty told me at that time how much he respected me and my family, and that he knew how sacred the Mor-mon faith was to us. Even though we didn't tell each other that we loved the other until we were in New York for the Heisman, still our feelings were pretty strong, and we wanted to move carefully in our relationship.

"I will have to admit that after Ty left my apartment that night, I was sure that he would never be back to take me out. There was just so much to do before we could date, especially with my family, and I felt that he would be so discouraged that we wouldn't get to date. After all, we had decided that we would have to establish certain rules. We had known each other as friends for three years, and we had too much respect for each other to date simply as a social thing.

"So at this time, even though I didn't really think I would see Ty again, we both agreed to the terms of our dating relationship. We knew that regardless of our reli-gious differences, we both shared the same moral values, and we would live by them."

Although I didn't know it at the time, she fasted and prayed about our relationship. She felt that if we began dating, it would move quite quickly because we were such close friends. She needed a confirmation so that she would be doing what the Lord had in mind for her.

I then set up an appointment with Mr. Herbert and traveled north to Salt Lake City, feeling even more anxious than I had felt before the Miami game. I wasn't too sure what I was going to say, but I knew it was a conversation I had to have, so I just trusted in his response.

Mr. Herbert remembers the conversation this way:

"Ty came to me early in October, and had the most sincere expression as he told me about his feelings for Kim and about his desire to date her. He said that he had to 'make things right' so that no one would get their feelings hurt. He was especially concerned for Misty, since they had previously dated.

"I was very proud of Ty, and the maturity he showed in handling the situation. Both InaLee and I expressed this to him, and told him that we would support his going out with Kim. We did tell Ty at this time about our expectations for all of our children to marry in the temple and to have a sound religious footing to their marriages. He said that he understood our values, and indicated that even though he was not a Latter-day Saint, he would learn more about the Church and see how it agreed with his own beliefs.

"InaLee and I then met with both girls and had a special conversation with them. We were relieved to hear Misty's response to Kim, which was, 'I'd rather have Ty as a brother-in-law than as a husband, so good luck, Kim.' We all laughed, and as parents of two wonderful daughters, we couldn't have been more proud."

I was really pleased with how our conversation went at the Herberts', and so when I finally asked Kim out, we both knew that things could be serious between us.

So it was that from the night of that first serious conversation about dating, Kim and I dated only each other. Our friendship deepened, and even though we didn't have much time together, we took advantage of what time we had.

MY FIRST MULE DEER

After getting back on track in winning our game with Colorado State, I was ready for a break. I was glad that we had the next weekend off, too, because that meant I could get back to the mountains and maybe get a deer.

Our trainer, George Curtis, invited me to hunt with him. My cousin Freddie Buchholz had come to Utah from Texas in hopes of getting a big buck, so he joined us. Actually, I was feeling pretty good about my hunting abilities, since I had just had my first successful elk hunt. I had gotten a nice spike bull, and so my confidence was up for the deer hunt.

The previous week I had gone on my first date with Kim, and so life was good. She even agreed to come up after our hunt for a live interview at our campsite for a local sports program.

During the hunt, Freddie was pretty excited to shoot a nice four-by-four buck, which is how we Texans refer to getting a four-point. I harvested one as well; but mine was smaller, although I hate to admit it. It was just a one-by-two, but at least it was a buck, and that meant I would have a good locker-full of meat for the winter.

FINISHING OUT THE SEASON

The following Saturday we hosted New Mexico for our homecoming game, and I was really happy that Andy Boyce and Derwin Gray did so well. Andy had a career day in receiving nine catches for 235 yards and two touchdowns. Derwin, on the other hand, picked off three Lobo passes and returned one of them seventeen yards for a touchdown. The final score was 55-31 in our favor.

Our next game was with Air Force in Colorado Springs, and because it is such a beautiful setting, I was really looking forward to playing there. When we arrived, however, an early winter storm was raging, so we had to prepare for a game in those conditions.

The snow was blowing throughout the game, and it was only twenty-seven degrees; but even so, Andy Boyce was able to have another career day, this time catching ten passes, three of which were for touchdowns. We won the game 54-7, and by this time we had a 7-1 overall record, with 5-0 in the conference.

We next went to War Memorial Stadium in Laramie and played Wyoming. The game was their first sellout in history, with over thirty-four thousand fans showing up. Again we were on national television, and unlike my first college game with Wyoming in which I threw for four interceptions, this time I passed for 484 yards and two touchdowns. We had a total offensive showing of 679 yards, so I was really happy for Peter Tuipulotu and Stacey Corley, our running backs.

On the following Saturday, we traveled north to Salt Lake City to try our luck against the Utes. They were building a solid program, and I personally had a lot of respect for them. I know there have been many comments about the "bad blood" between the two schools, but I enjoyed the rivalry. I had learned that what was now the University of Utah had been founded under President Brigham Young's leadership about twenty-five years before he founded the Y; so I figured that with similar beginnings we should have a good, friendly competition.

We were behind 10-7 in the first quarter, but rallied to beat Utah 45-22. This win gave us the WAC championship, and I felt good that we had achieved this goal. I really loved to play Utah, whether in Salt Lake City or Provo, and I was happy that I had been able to pass for 451 yards and five touchdowns.

With each game, I was learning that even though my own stats were quite good, they would be nothing without the total contribution of the rest of the team. My teammates made me look good, but I sincerely believe that it was their attitude and their work ethic that made it all happen.

We came back to Cougar Stadium the following Saturday and beat Utah State by a score of 45-10. Passing for 560 yards allowed me to break the NCAA record, set the previous year by Houston's Andre Ware, for most passing yards in a season (at that point I had 4,869, and would finish out the season with 5,188 yards). That was a great feeling, and again I can't say enough about the playing of our receivers—Andy Boyce, Chris Smith, and Brent Nyberg. I was also grateful for our outstanding offensive line, consisting of Neal Fort, Mike Keim, Bob Stephens, Jim Balmforth, and Bryan May. Along with the defense that kept getting the ball back for us, these guys were the ones who made my job easy and fun.

At least my job was easy and fun when we *won.* We didn't have that good fortune the last week of the season, however, as Hawaii beat us 59-28. I talked about that game in chapter 1 of this book, so I won't say too much about it here. I will say that Hawaii deserved to win with the way their quarterback, Garrett Gabriel, and their running back Dane McArthur played. In looking back on it, I think that our having just won the Heisman, as well as our already having won the WAC title, just didn't give us the motivation we needed to play our best. We did come back from a 35-14 deficit at halftime to trail by just 41-28 at the end of the third quarter. But that wasn't good enough, as the Rainbows reeled off eighteen more points in the fourth quarter.

DECEMBER, THE HEISMAN, AND HOLIDAY BOWL XIII

December was one of the most memorable months of my life. I was especially happy for Coach Edwards and the coaching staff, with the recognition that was now given to our program—for I knew of the many years they spent building the program on a foundation of excellence. I think they were able to do this because they stressed our getting an education first, and then put athletics in its proper perspective.

After Kim and I returned to Utah from receiving the Heisman, our relationship took on new dimensions almost every day. As Mrs. Herbert (which was still what I called her at that time) remembers it: "When Ty brought home the Heisman watch and hat to Frank, and treated our family as he did, we knew things were getting serious between Ty and Kim. I smiled at my husband and said, 'Frank, he's just trying to make points with you.' Frank was cute, as he replied, 'Yes, InaLee, and it's working!'

"So we accepted the things he brought from New York as a form of fun bribery for our allowing him to date Kim. But seriously, Frank and I have always had the highest amount of trust and respect for Ty, and we knew he and Kim would make the right decision, if they were to marry. It was really a happy Christmas season for our entire family."

So while things got back to a semi-normal condition, as Kim and I prepared for our final exams, in my heart I knew that my future was becoming more clear to me every day. We dated regularly, and often our thoughts would center around religion and our respective viewpoints regarding it. Kim respected me for what I believed, and I think she dated me in the first place because of my own standards—which didn't really differ from her own. But still she seemed anxious as we attended each other's church services, and yet I appreciated how she didn't push me toward joining the Mormon church.

Christmas was great. Kim gave me a nice jacket and a golden retriever puppy we named Presley. My roommate

Rick Evans had owned a dog that he named Elvis, so now it was my turn, and I thought I should just finish things off with the name Presley. Presley has since then become a good hunting dog, and loves to get out in the mountains and fields with me.

After I had received my gifts, I gave Kim a pearl ring and a black leather coat. And I might add that she looked good wearing both gifts!

Final exams were finally over, and I was glad to get on the plane and fly to San Diego. I knew that our team was pretty beat up physically, and that worried me. But I also knew that we would have a great week, and that regardless of the outcome of the game with Texas A&M, we would have had a good season.

Texas A&M was led by a great quarterback, Bucky Richardson, and an All-American running back, Darren Lewis, so I knew the game would be difficult. I also knew they would be gunning for us because they hadn't gotten the press we had, and if they could beat us they would end their season on a very positive note.

I had a slight separation of my right shoulder, which I had gotten in the Utah game, and Matt Bellini, Tony Crutchfield, and Norm Dixon didn't even suit up. Besides that, quite a few of our other players were playing with smaller injuries, and so we knew the game would be an uphill battle.

The game was tied 7-7 through most of the first quarter, and then just before the end of that quarter, A&M scored again to make it 14-7. Then they scored twenty-three unanswered second-quarter points, and we went into the locker room feeling pretty beat up, since they had a 37-7 halftime lead. What made it even worse for me was the fact that I had just incurred a separation in my left shoulder. It felt pretty bad.

Unfortunately, the worst was yet to come.

The big story for me came at the beginning of the third quarter, when A&M's William Thomas put a crunching sack on me that totally separated my right shoulder, adding to the previous tear from the Utah game. I left the game at that point, and wondered many times throughout the rest of the game if I was going to have to go through surgery. I was also worried about whether I could hold up my rifle, since Dad and I were scheduled to go hunting a few days later. It was a painful, depressing hour for me all the way around.

A&M won the game by a score of 65-14. That was a crushing defeat for our team, but Coach Edwards and his staff put things in perspective by being more concerned about our injuries, and our season, than about the final score. No one likes to lose like that; but we accepted it, and the team flew home for the new year, knowing that even with the three losses we had suffered, the season had been outstanding in many ways. I felt good that it had brought a lot of respect and recognition to Brigham Young University and to our football program.

The Two Most Important Decisions of My Life

THE HOLIDAY BOWL, WITH MY FOLKS

In addition to the football game, being in San Diego for the Holiday Bowl presented another opportunity for me that was very important. It provided a time for me to sit down with my parents and let them know what was happening between me and Kim.

Up to this point in my life, I hadn't really looked into the Mormon church as a way of life for me. I had greatly admired its moral teachings and how the gospel stressed family togetherness, but still I hadn't begun studying its beliefs in depth. I *had* taken the required religion courses each semester, and so I was pretty well acquainted with the Latter-day Saint beliefs and doctrines. And this, along with what Kim and my other friends had taught me, gave me a positive respect for the Church. Eric Mortensen, my roommate, was an especially good example to me, and would always live the beliefs of the Church, no matter what.

By the time I was set to have the conversation with my folks about Kim, I had a fairly good understanding of what she believed. I knew she would never force her religion on me, but I had such respect for her and for the other Latter-day Saints who had become my closest friends, that I wanted to know for myself if their church was true, and if I could fully accept its teachings.

Kim and I had always joked about our differences, too. When Kim had asked me earlier in the fall if I would be willing to take the missionary discussions, I responded by telling her that I would if she would be willing to take the Methodist discussions. I didn't know if the Methodist church had any conversion discussions, but I figured that we ought to be on equal footing here, so I teased her about that.

Now the hour had arrived.

I went out to eat with my folks before Kim arrived in San Diego, and afterward we went to their hotel room to visit. Mom was pretty tired, though, and she fell asleep. I think this may have been her way of allowing my dad and me to visit father-to-son.

Before long I got right to the point, and told my dad that I thought Kim was the one for me to marry. His response was positive: "Yes, I told your mother that I thought Kim was the one, and we want you to know that we approve. Betty and I have always enjoyed Kim's sense of humor. She comes from a good family, and we just love her, and think she'll fit right into our family.

"After all," Dad said, smiling, "when we played whiffle ball last summer, I found out she could hit pretty hard and run fast, so with all of her other qualities, she'll make a great daughter-in-law."

I knew this was a coach talking, and we laughed about that game of whiffle ball. It had taken place after the Freedom Festival parade, when our family had met and picnicked with the Herbert family at River Grove Park in north Provo.

I then told my dad that I wanted to look into the Mormon faith, and see which way we wanted to go with that. I had been taught that religious unity was important in the home, and I wanted him to know that I was not considering this lightly.

I then changed the subject and asked Dad about how I should go about purchasing an engagement ring, and all the things that went into proposing marriage to Kim. He suggested that I purchase one in Provo, and that perhaps the jeweler could work out a payment plan with me.

This was a good visit, and again I was reminded of how great my parents were and how much faith and trust they had in my agency. They had reared me to be honest with my feelings and to be true to what I felt; and their response to my feelings about Kim at this time only confirmed in my mind how lucky I was to have them as my parents.

TO TEXAS AND SURGERY

Following the Holiday Bowl, I returned to Texas with my parents. I knew that I would likely have at least one shoulder operated on, and it was quite a painful trip. My dad had previously coached a friend, Bud Curtis, who was now a practicing physician in San Antonio. Dr. Curtis and his partner, Dr. DeLee, took X rays, and we discussed the various options, especially with regard to the right shoulder. They felt that the left one would heal normally, and my parents and I made the decision to proceed with the right one.

HUNTING WITH SONNY

After my surgery had been scheduled, my dad and I drove to Laredo, where we hunted deer. I was pretty sore and knew I wouldn't be doing much hunting, but I really wanted to go. I knew I couldn't mess my shoulders up any more than they already were, so it wasn't really a risk.

We spent the night, and then Dad got up for a good breakfast the following morning. It consisted of breakfast tacos, which were made of eggs, sausage, and potatoes mixed together. They call them "taquitos" in Texas. It was the best breakfast in the world, and my mouth just drooled because I couldn't eat anything before my scheduled surgery that evening. The food smelled good, but I knew what I had to do.

Anyway, we began our hunt. I had attached a small tripod on the barrel of my rifle, thinking that if I saw a deer I could just have the rifle sitting on the hood of the car and shoot from there. But while I didn't even see a deer, Dad got a nice buck that day, with a full 19-inch rack. It wasn't a trophy buck as mine had been a few years earlier, but then he never did have my kind of luck. It was nice, though, and I helped him feel good about it.

We laughed, and he reminded me that *he* was the one who had sacrificed by giving Koy and me the good positions the morning we bagged our trophy bucks. We really enjoyed ourselves on that hunt, even though it was cut short because of my scheduled surgery.

On our way home, we stopped in Freer, Texas, and again he ate—this time another of my favorite foods, Texas fajitas. It was bar-be-cued just right, and he ordered it to go.

When we got outside of town, Dad pulled over. Knowing that I couldn't eat, he then asked me to drive so that he *could* eat. Again I was in sheer agony, as I drove with sore shoulders and an empty stomach while Dad once again "tanked up" on all that good food.

THE OPERATION

We finally arrived back home, and before I knew it I was getting ready for my trip to the hospital. I called Kim before leaving home, and she gave me her support, which made me feel better. I then entered the hospital under the assumed name of Tim Newman, because we hadn't released the news of the surgery to the press. We wanted it to be dealt with privately so that I could get more rest the day following the surgery while I was still in the hospital.

The operation was successful, and before I knew it I was again conscious and beginning to heal. I was glad to have made the decision to take care of things while the injury was still fresh, and looking back on it, the decision was a good one. My throwing arm rotates perfectly, as though the separation had never taken place.

TO UTAH AND KIM

A week later, after returning from Texas, I wasted no time following up on Dad's counsel about getting engaged. I went to my friend Dave Payne, who owned Payne's Jewelry, and he taught me about the different quality in diamonds. I finally decided on a beautiful diamond stone. Dave then arranged terms for me so that I could pay on it monthly. After I made the down payment, he said he would put the diamond in a temporary setting so that I could give it to Kim. Then together we could pick out a setting she would like.

I had to wait a week to get the loaner setting, and by that time I was getting pretty anxious. I wanted to be formally *engaged,* so I wasn't too long on patience.

I was really in love, I think for the very first time, and when Kim had first told me that she loved *me,* she also said that I was the very first person she had told that to. I knew she had dated a lot of guys during our college years, so her words meant even that much more to me. I knew where I stood, and I was happy to know that our feelings were new and were deeper and more meaningful than ever before. It would be a good basis for our marriage.

POPPING THE MILLION-DOLLAR QUESTION

Right after this, we decided to attend a Utah Jazz-San Antonio Spurs basketball game in the Salt Palace. I had grown up in San Antonio, of course, so I was really a Spurs fan. Kim, on the other hand, was a Jazz fan all the way.

So we went to Salt Lake City and attended the game. The Jazz won by about twenty points, and just killed the Spurs, which put Kim in a pretty excited frame of mind. I thought I might separate my shoulder again, the way I was always pulling her back into her seat during the game. She was really into it.

On our way back to Provo, she turned to me and said, "Ty, can I ask you something?"

"Yeah, go ahead," I replied, not sure where she was going in the conversation.

"No, I don't think I will . . ."

"Come on," I said, "you can't back out of it now. Just ask your question."

The date was January 15, and I had already asked her the night before if she would go out to dinner with me that coming Thursday. I knew the ring—would be ready then, so I wanted the evening to be special.

Finally Kim decided to ask her question. "Just what is this pearl ring for, Ty? Someone asked me the other day if it was a friendship ring, a promise ring, or just what it meant."

I answered by saying, "Now, Kim, you're ruining everything."

"What did I do?" she asked, all innocent-like.

"I guess I'm just going to have to tell you. I bought a diamond, and it's getting mounted. That's why I asked you out on Thursday, so . . . will you marry me?"

We were in my Blazer, which had bucket seats, and besides that my right shoulder was in a sling. So I was driving with my left hand, and I couldn't even put my arm around her. I just had to ask the question.

We were traveling south on I-15 and were about at the state prison facilities when I popped the question. But she just stared at me, without speaking, and I was beginning to wonder if it might be better for me to be on the other side of the fence that was between us and the prison.

Finally, not being able to take the silence any longer, I said, "Kim, you don't have to answer me now. You can wait until Thursday, if you want to."

But she didn't hesitate when I said that. Instead, she said, "Yes, Ty, I'll marry you. I don't have to wait until Thursday."

Boy, was I ever relieved! The hard part was over, and before I knew what was happening, she climbed over onto the console and gave me a big hug and kiss.

The rest of the ride home was quiet, as we were both pretty much into our own thoughts. We were happy, though, and we both felt that we were moving in the right direction.

Later that night, after dropping Kim off at her apartment, I headed back up to my home in Orem. I thought then about Kim's religious convictions, and I greatly admired her personal beliefs. I really wanted to know for myself about the Mormon church, and I didn't want Kim to influence my decision about whether to join—one way or the other. I knew that if I gained a testimony of the Church's truthfulness, I would become a member, regardless of whom I married. If I joined the Church I would join because of my feelings about *it,* and I think she respected me for that.

GIVING KIM THE RING

On Thursday evening, I showed up on Kim's doorstep with a dozen long-stemmed red roses, and she was pretty happy when she answered the door.

We then left her apartment and went on our formal

engagement date, eating dinner at the Oak Crest Inn near the mouth of Spanish Fork Canyon.

I thought I would have some fun with the evening, so before picking Kim up I took the ring box out of the white box it had come in, and replaced the smaller box with a penny. I placed the box containing the penny on the seat of the car, thinking Kim would notice it when she sat down. But she didn't, so I put the box up on the dash and rattled it, the whole time smiling at her. That got her attention, so I told her that she could look in the box, if she really wanted to. "Are you sure?" she asked, smiling all tentative-like. "Yeah," I said, "go ahead."

Kim remembers it this way: "I looked at the box, I became excited, and my eyes got really big! So I opened the box, and when I saw the penny, I looked over at Ty and said, 'You big tease!' We were still laughing as we went into the restaurant to eat. That helped us both relax and enjoy the evening."

Finally, as we were finishing the main course, I excused myself to go to the bathroom. Kim was unsuspecting by this time, so instead of going into the bathroom I went into the kitchen and gave the ring to our waitress. I then returned to my seat, and in a minute our dessert, the Mud Slide, was served—ring and all. It was a great way to end the evening.

The next day we set a dinner date with Kim's folks to announce our engagement to them. On our way to their home to pick them up, we had our engagement pictures taken at a place where three of the Herbert sisters worked. We then took Kim's folks to dinner at a nice restaurant in town. They were really happy for us.

One of the four of us talked almost the whole time, although I won't say which one of us that was. But whichever one it was, that person talked about love and commitment and things like that, and the rest of us pretty much listened. Kim was nervous for me, having to listen to so much counsel, but I was handling it okay and enjoyed the meal. I knew that a father has the right to become protective when his first daughter announces her plans to get married and leave home.

BECOMING A LATTER-DAY SAINT

When we returned to Kim's apartment that evening, we began to talk about the temple and all of the things associated with marrying for eternity. At this time I told Kim that I already had an appointment set with the missionaries for the following night, and I asked her if she would take the discussions with me. I told her that I had already talked with our trainer, George Curtis, about taking the missionary discussions in his home, so it was all planned out.

The next night we did meet with the missionaries and with the Curtises, and it was then that I began to feel something new. I felt good about what I was learning.

It was during the third discussion, actually, that I realized for the first time where I stood with the Church. I knew that I was the same person who had left Texas, in terms of my standards and my desire to live a good, Christian life. I was also thankful that my friends had let me search out the Church on my own, without forcing it on me. So now, for the first time, I was feeling that there *was* something more. Not really something *different* than what I had been taught growing up, but something that would add to what I already knew to be true.

I realize now that it was the Spirit of the Lord working on me, because my thoughts and feelings were coming together in a way I had never known. I told the missionaries that night that I had made up my mind, and that I would become a member of the Church.

Not only could I see, mentally, that the Church of Jesus Christ had been restored to the earth by Joseph Smith—that he really *was* a prophet of God—but I was beginning to *feel* the truthfulness of it, as well. I had never known a feeling like it, and because my parents and grandparents had always taught me to live right and then trust my feelings, I began to see that being baptized into The Church of Jesus Christ of Latter-day Saints was the only course I could take. I then selected the sixth of February as the day that I would become a member of the Church, and as we prayed, both Kim and I felt that I would be ready.

Before we knew it, February sixth arrived. It would be a day that would mark my entering into the waters of baptism and then coming back out a new person. I was quite nervous, but my teammate Peter Tuipulotu was also being baptized in the same services, so that made it easier. Peter had been investigating the Church for some time, and had worn out a couple of sets of missionaries. But he was now ready, and his testimony helped mine as we prepared for this date together.

Our baptismal service was held in a chapel in Lindon, the little town where George Curtis lived and where I had taken the discussions. On our way down off the hill, as we headed toward the chapel, I became quite nervous and wondered if I was making the right decision.

A few moments later, when the meeting began, I felt the right spirit there, and I knew I was doing what the Lord expected of me. Even though we thought only a few people would know about the services, there were over three hundred in attendance. We held the meeting in the chapel—with the missionaries, Elders Turpin and Carlton, offering the opening and closing prayers. We had developed a special friendship throughout the discussions, and I was happy they could attend. Coach Edwards also attended with his wife, Patti, and he was the main speaker before the baptisms actually took place.

A group of Polynesian men sang in honor of Peter. Then Kim's seventeen-year-old sister, Stacie, sang "His Hands" by Kenneth Cope. Kim's mother had put together a slide presentation on the life of Christ; so while Stacie sang, the chapel was darkened and we all enjoyed the presentation. Following this program, a few close friends and family members went into the baptistry—first with Peter, and then with me—to witness our baptisms.

Because Kim's mom and dad were like second parents to me, I had asked her father, Frank Herbert, to baptize me. I knew that he honored his priesthood and that he would be in a position to use this power to act for God worthily, and he graciously accepted.

When we were walking down into the water, dressed in white, I'll have to admit that I was quite nervous. Brother Herbert whispered to me at that time, "How long can you hold your breath?" We smiled, and I knew he was just trying to get me to relax. I was looking foward to being baptized in the same manner of the Savior's baptism, so after the prayer was offered, I was completely immersed.

I then came out of the water, fully cleansed. It felt good, knowing that my sins had been washed away. Even though I couldn't see Kim, I knew that she was really happy for me, and for *us*.

After we had changed clothes and were back in the chapel, Peter and I were confirmed members of the Church through the laying on of hands. Coach Claude Bassett confirmed me. Through the power of the priesthood held by him as well as by those assisting him, I was then given the gift of the Holy Ghost.

Although I didn't fully understand this gift at the time, since then I have often felt special gratitude for the help I have received from the Holy Spirit. I know that this Spirit guides our lives and helps us make correct decisions, and I never want to take it for granted.

After we were confirmed, Peter and I were then given the opportunity of sharing our testimonies. When I spoke, I told everyone that my parents had taught me to be a Christian all my life, and that I had tried to conduct myself as one. I told the audience that I hadn't joined the Church because of Kim, although knowing her had given me a better opportunity to become acquainted with the teachings of the Church. I then expressed my happiness, and added that I knew that Jesus Christ was my Savior. That was saying a whole lot for me, so I closed my remarks about then and sat down. This was probably the hardest part of the meeting for me, but I was glad to have shared my thoughts at that time.

I need to insert here that the second time I shared my conversion story, at a fireside a few weeks later, I said, "I know that Jesus is a prophet . . ." Then I realized what I had said, and I recovered somewhat by saying, "Of course he's a prophet, but I know he is the Christ." Sharing these sacred things took a little getting used to, but I knew that I grew from each experience, so I didn't mind.

Before continuing with my description of the evening I became a Church member, I want to also relate an interview I had with a fellow from *USA Today* a few days later while I was waiting for a flight at the Salt Lake International Airport. He asked me if I had joined the Church for Kim. I politely told him that I hadn't. I explained that I hadn't joined the Church of Kim, but had joined the Church of Christ. I was sincere in what I said, and I think he believed me. I later called Kim and told her what I had said. I didn't want her to be upset. We laughed about it, though, and everything was fine.

Going back to the evening of my joining the Church—following the baptismal services, we all went over to Roger and Dahnelle Overly's home. Dahnelle is Brother Herbert's sister. We ate ice cream and enjoyed visiting there.

My only regret was that *my* family couldn't have spent the evening with me. Even though they were fifteen hundred miles away, I felt close to them, and knew that they were respectful of my wanting to continue to enjoy the Savior's influence in my life.

Earlier that day I had received the engagement ring back from Dave Payne, with the setting Kim had selected, so I gave it to her at that time. It was the perfect way to celebrate what was, to that point, the happiest day of my life.

That night as I climbed into bed, I knew that I had joined the Church for the right reasons, and now I looked forward to spending the eternities with Kim and with children we would one day be given.

WHEN TO MARRY

From that day forward, Kim and I began to talk more and more about a wedding date: Should we marry in a civil ceremony before my senior year and be sealed in the temple later? Or should we wait until the anniversary of my baptism so that we could then marry in the temple? One of my big concerns was my parents and grandparents; they had been through quite a bit the past year, with my sister Dee's having had a stillborn baby, and with Paw Paw's failing health.

I think my life had also been a big burden for my folks in that they had given up their own privacy since my winning the Heisman. They had received quite a bit of negative mail about my joining the Church, with people they didn't even know telling them that they had lost me as a son. It was a difficult time for them, even though they were respectful of my joining the Church and marrying Kim.

I need to mention, too, that Kim had long since fallen in love with my parents and family. She was always telling me how great they were, and how thankful I should be for the way they had reared me. Her words of love and support toward my grandparents and parents—as well as Koy and my sisters—have always meant a lot to me. But I especially appreciated her words at that time.

PAW PAW'S DEATH

About a month after my baptism, Paw Paw passed
away. Just prior to his death, my sister Dee Dorman had
delivered her first baby, a stillbirth. At the time, I had
flown to Ft. Worth to receive the Davey O'Brien Award,
and my folks were supposed to come up and receive it
with me. But when I arrived at the hotel, Dad called and
was sad to report Dee's condition.

So, without my folks, I received the award that night,
then flew back to Utah the following morning. I then
took Kim and we drove right back to south Texas to be
with Dee and her husband, Steve, and to attend the funeral.

So Kim, who was planning on joining our family, was
able to meet Paw Paw and get to know him and Maw
Maw at that time. He passed away a month later, and
Kim and I have always been glad that she had been able
to spend time at his bedside. This was the last time either of us saw him alive.

During this final visit, I reflected on the Heisman
event four months earlier and how happy Paw Paw had
been for me. He was even happier when my dad took the
Heisman Trophy back to Texas and gave it to Paw Paw.
He and Maw Maw had kept most of my earlier trophies,
and I knew how much this had meant to him. Even
though I hadn't been there to present the trophy to Paw
Paw myself, my dad had told me that he became quite
emotional when he received it. He and Maw Maw have
given me so much happiness and support through my
life that this was the very least I could do for them.

When I went back down to Texas for Paw Paw's funeral, I had the opportunity of letting my parents know
that they hadn't lost me as a son, but that I was the
same person they had reared me to be. I was concerned
for them, and really wanted them to be part of our marriage. Kim was very understanding of my feelings, and

even though she had always prepared for a temple marriage, she knew that our situation was complex.

So I told my folks at that time that we would do what we felt was best, and I appreciated their support.

DECIDING THROUGH PRAYER

Returning home and to our future plans, Kim and I felt that perhaps we should visit with President Thomas S. Monson of the First Presidency of the Church. He had been very close to the Herbert family, and because of my circumstances, he had offered to visit with us if and when we had a need. So we called and made an appointment, and went to Salt Lake City to meet with him.

President Monson is a true man of God, and Kim and I could feel his unusual spirit when we shook his hand.

He offered us seats, and as we shared with him our dilemma about when to get married, he gave us some sound counsel. He didn't tell us what he thought we should do, but instead just suggested that we find out what the Lord wanted us to do. It was a very helpful meeting, and Kim and I left his office knowing that we would be directed in making the right choice.

Finally, after thinking and praying about things, we both decided that it would be best to get married that summer. President Monson had read to us the policy of the Church regarding temple marriage. It stated that when a convert is married civilly within a year of his baptism, he can later be sealed in the temple on the anniversary of the baptism. This meant that we could proceed with our wedding that summer. We could then enjoy as a couple our final year at the Y, and all of the trips associated with my changing football career. We also knew that this time would allow me to prepare for my receiving the Melchizedek Priesthood and being ordained to the office of an elder. We could then be sealed on or around February 6, the anniversary of my baptism.

Our decision felt right for us, and both Kim's and my parents supported us in it. We knew that we would be worthy of a temple marriage at the time of our wedding, even though we would have to wait out the year in order for me to be prepared to be ordained an elder in the priesthood. This ordination had to take place before I could go to the temple and be sealed to Kim. The important thing for me was to grow in my testimony and in my priesthood, and to be the kind of husband Kim had always planned on marrying.

Even thinking about that made me feel good. No longer did I have to worry about just myself and my own feelings. I had now made a commitment to marry the most beautiful girl in the world, and I wanted to make her happy.

A HECTIC ENGAGEMENT

I don't know how Kim held up so well, but the entire time we were engaged was spent with me traveling around the country, attending award ceremonies, both of us taking classes, speaking at firesides, and so forth. It was a heavy schedule, but Kim kept me organized and headed in the right direction, so it all seemed to work out for us.

I have to say that I received a great deal of support from my professors at this time, too. They would allow me to make my work up if I had to miss class, and because of their help, by the time the semester ended I had earned over a 3.0 grade point average. Looking back on that semester, as well as my other experiences, I would have to say that when I am the busiest, I am also the most productive. It's a good lesson for me to remember later on in life.

OUR WEDDING

On June 23, two weeks before the wedding, all of my family arrived from Texas. The Herberts were gracious, opening their home to all of us, and it was something else. In addition to the Herberts' large family being there, Maw Maw came up with my parents, as well as my brother, Koy, and my sister Lori. My sister Dee and her husband, Steve, also drove up with my high school bud John Martinez, and they stayed there as well. In all, about seventeen of us were living under one roof for two weeks, and everyone seemed to get along well. It was really a good time for our families to get to know each other, and believe me—we did!

I had a summer job with the Provo City Department of Economic Development, and so I would commute down to work each day and then come back up to stay with everyone each night. I slept in the room with Kim's little brother Richard, and because he and I had become such close friends, this was a lot of fun. Kim was working for Cannon Industries in Salt Lake City, and we were both trying to save up enough money to make it through our senior year together.

MOM'S SUDDEN ILLNESS

Several weeks before the wedding, my mom had found out that she had cancer. This had been quite a blow to all of us, but she had picked up our spirits and kept us going. She began her chemotherapy treatments, and I think this is when I learned how strong a person my mother is. She knew she could beat it, and didn't want us feeling sorry for her.

Mom was right in the middle of her chemotherapy treatments when she had to leave for Utah and the final preparations before the wedding. Because Kim's mother,

InaLee, also had had cancer and had taken the chemotherapy treatments, my mom went to InaLee's doctor and continued her treatment in Salt Lake City. Kim and I have always felt that our mothers were a lot alike, and this was a time for them to really get to know each other.

Kim's folks had just moved into their home two weeks before my family arrived from Texas, and although boxes were everywhere, we were pretty much one big happy family.

We did have one giant catastrophe, though, and that was the flooding of their basement. There was quite a bit of excitement, and when Mr. Herbert saw what had happened, with the water everywhere, he used a few colorful adjectives that I teased him about. We all laughed, then waded into the water with mops and brooms and buckets, and after quite a bit of work, we got it cleaned up.

Kim and I had rented a small home in Pleasant Grove from our good friends, Renae and Bill; so before the wedding, we all went down and picked cherries from the trees in the backyard. Our families were all happy for us, and we could hardly wait to move into our first home.

Finally, after what seemed like forever, July 2 finally arrived. The Herberts' bishop, Thomas Liddell, of the Little Cottonwood Ward, had agreed to marry us, and all the other arrangements had been made.

The ceremony took place in the Latter-day Saint chapel just north of Temple Square, and there was really a special spirit there. Kim and I were thankful to be with both of our families, and after all we had gone through, neither of us could hardly believe that we now belonged together.

Following the wedding ceremony, Kim and I went out to the Herberts' chapel in Sandy. Their ward Relief Society sisters had prepared a delicious wedding brunch for our family and close friends. Bryan May, one of my offensive linemen, had a sister in the ward by the name of Marla Holbrook. So Marla, along with her mother and sisters and others from the ward, worked long and hard to do this for us. We felt that we needed a setting like this so that we could have our privacy. We'll always be thankful for the effort these ladies put forth for us.

THE RECEPTION AT THE TRIAD CENTER

The wedding reception finally took place, and after changing in the Devereaux House, we had pictures taken out on the lawn. Our colors were black and white, and so even though the men looked like a group of penguins, the ladies looked beautiful. The press was everywhere, which made it kind of awkward, but we tried to be accommodating.

Finally our line formed, and it all began. Coach Edwards had given us advice earlier in the day on how to get four thousand people through the reception line, and even though he didn't get paid for it, we appreciated his coaching advice. Always a coach in true form. Taking this advice, we had Kim's three uncles—J. C., Stan, and Roger Cook—as well as Rick Anderson and Steve Bartlett all assist in ushering the people quickly through the line, which consisted of Kim's parents; my parents; my ushers, Steve Dorman, Scott Charlton, Eric Mortensen, and Dave and Richard Herbert; my best man, Koy; me and Kim; Misty, the maid of honor; the bridesmaids, Dee, Stacie, Lisa, and Lori; Maw Maw; Kim's grandfathers, Ross Cook and Leo Herbert; and two flower girls, Andrea Bartlett and Melissa Cook.

The line itself also included a replica of Kim's brother Mike, who was on a mission in Perth, Australia. We put a tuxedo on a life-size mannequin and attached to it a cardboard head with a picture of Mike's face blown up to life-size. He had sent us a tape with his best wishes on it, so we attached a small cassette recorder behind the head of the mannequin, and it played continuously throughout the evening. The message said, "G'day, mate. I'm Mike. Pleased to meet you." Folks really got a kick out of that, and we were happy that Mike was able to vicariously participate in the wedding with us. One elderly lady did have some problems with the mannequin, though. She kept talking to it, but of course it would only repeat the taped message, which she wasn't able to hear. Dave was standing next to the mannequin, and finally the lady tapped him on the arm and said, "Excuse me, but this young man won't talk to me." We all laughed when we heard about this experience, even though we felt bad for the elderly lady.

So, all in all, twenty-one of us formed the line, and we weren't sure if we felt more sorry for ourselves or for those who had to come through the line. For four and a half hours we stood there, and by the time it ended, several pairs of legs and feet were numb! But we all laughed and enjoyed ourselves, so it was worth it. By the end of the evening, 3,800 friends and family had signed the guest book and shaken our hands.

As Kim and I were preparing to leave the reception, I thought back to my original conversation with her father. He had stressed the goals of his family to be together forever. Now, as I looked at the Herberts and the Detmers running around trying to gather things up, I realized how insignificant all the football medals and honors were. Instead, I felt such love for them all that I just wanted Kim and me to be a family with them forever.

I knew that the kind of family I had come from, as well as Kim's family that I was marrying into, were the quality people that would enjoy each other as a single unit forever. I knew then that I could not have been blessed to have been born into a finer family. And now, with those numbers growing, I was happier than I had ever thought possible. I knew that Kim felt the same way, and we could hardly wait to begin our lives together.

SPEAKING IN TEXAS ON THE FOURTH OF JULY

The morning following the reception, we went out to the Herberts' home, and there we opened the gifts people had been kind enough to give us. This was a pretty humbling experience for both Kim and me, and we realized then how thoughtful everyone had been.

That afternoon we flew to McAllen, Texas, to fulfill a commitment I had made to the people there. We had been asked to be the grand marshall in the Fourth of July parade there, and to then speak two different times in connection with the festivities.

We had a great time doing this and being with those good-hearted Texans; but we found that things don't always work out as they're planned.

Our expenses were significant, and had been paid by the people in McAllen. But the NCAA contacted us and informed us that we would have to pay back the money for the expenses we incurred on the trip. (If the people had given me a plaque or an award—and if this award had been given to recipients over the previous five years—there would have been no violation of NCAA rules. But there was no award; we were just participating in the town's celebration of the birth of our nation. So it was declared a violation.) There was really no place to pay back the money, since the tickets had been complimentary; so we had to give the money to a charity. We chose the United Way, and because we didn't have the money in cash, we had to take out a loan for the right amount and pay it to the charity immediately, or we would be in violation of NCAA rules.

OPEN HOUSE IN HOUSTON

Kim and I later found out that after we had left Salt

Lake City for McAllen, our families had packed up and had driven straight through to San Antonio. My sister Dee and her husband, Steve, had left about three hours before the others because they wanted to get back early.

Before the two families started out in their caravan, they had family prayer and asked for protection in their journey so that nothing would go wrong.

About two in the morning, when the caravan was traveling along near Shiprock, New Mexico, on the Indian reservation, they suddenly looked over and saw another car coming up alongside their cars. The folks were surprised when they recognized the people in the car coming up alongside theirs as being Dee and Steve. When they all stopped, they found that Dee and Steve had experienced a blowout of one of their tires, out in the middle of nowhere. For two hours they had been praying that the caravan would come along to help them out. They had a little "doughnut" spare tire, and they had put it on their car—but they had had no money to get another tire, so when the folks came along, their prayers were answered.

Later, Dee and Steve told Kim and me that when they told their story, Maw Maw had said to them, "Well, if you hadn't been in such an all-fire big hurry to get on the road, you could have traveled with us. We had a prayer that nothing would go wrong with us, and nothing has."

They did find a town, and bought a new tire. And, before too many more hours, they all safely arrived in San Antonio.

Following Kim's and my two-day visit in McAllen, the airlines rerouted us to Houston, and we had a reception there with all of my relatives. We were out on a ranch which belonged to my mom's uncle, Ed Hartman, and his wife, Bea.

Many of my family members had worked hard to make this an enjoyable "southern hospitality" time for us, and we were grateful for their efforts.

Kim had an experience when she went shopping at a local mall with her mother and sisters, as well as my sisters, Dee and Lori. Kim became separated from the others, and it wasn't until three hours later that she was finally located. She had purchased a couple of things when they first parted company, and then had spent the final two and a half hours visiting with a policeman in the parking lot. When her mother asked her why she had done this, Kim said, "Well, Ty gave me a hundred dollars to spend, but I felt guilty after spending eighty dollars, so I decided to spend my time in the parking lot. That way I knew I wouldn't be spending the rest of our money."

Kim has always been thoughtful that way, and even aspired at one time to become an attorney. She is a very good money manager, and I realized right away this added bonus to the person I would spend my life with.

When they returned from shopping, we had a real Texas bar-be-cue. We also played rag ball in a field soaked with water, and everybody was covered with mud, having the time of their lives.

That night we stayed out at the Hartmans' beach house on Galveston Island, and we really enjoyed that. As Kim says, it was pretty romantic—even though the families were there with us.

I did have one accident that night that was pretty hard on me. The beach house we stayed in was built on stilts, and the concrete pad for a garage was below it. Anyway, I dropped my Heisman watch down through a crack on the balcony, and it landed on that concrete pad, with springs and other parts flying everywhere. It totally ruined the watch. Luckily for me, when I was a Heisman finalist the following year, they gave each of us an even better watch than the first one I had received. But at the time it was pretty disheartening for me to have broken the original Heisman watch.

Even though this put a damper on things, we had

enjoyed a great evening with my family and relatives, and we were grateful for all of their efforts in our behalf.

A HONEYMOON—SORT OF

At the conclusion of the wedding festivities, Kim and I got back on the plane for our trip back to Utah. We barely arrived when we had to leave for Hawaii and the annual WAC media conference, which was to be held on the island of Maui. Each year, one or two players from each WAC school are asked to attend the conference and to be interviewed by the various media personnel. Director Tuckett, Coach Edwards, and Ralph Zobell would also be there, and we would enjoy the conference with them.

But because Kim and I were still trying to find a couple of days to be alone together, I paid her expenses and we went three days early, staying in Oahu on Waikiki Beach. It felt good not to be there to play a football game, and we were able to relax in the sun.

We then flew over to Maui and became guests of the WAC officials. They were very accommodating, and even though our time was not really our own, we enjoyed the different, and to us more spectacular, beauty of that island.

Finally, at the conclusion of the conference, we left the tropical islands of Hawaii, hoping to one day return when we could just be by ourselves and enjoy Hawaii as it should be enjoyed. We were exhausted, but we had just completed one of the happiest years of our lives. We knew of the demands that were being placed on our time, but we were eager to get settled in our little rental home in Pleasant Grove—and to begin enjoying life together. It was a day, and a year, we will always remember.

Senior Year—a Real Character Builder

A FINAL SEASON OF PLAYING COLLEGE FOOTBALL

As our team prepared for my fifth and final season at the Y, I knew that things would be hard. We had a tough schedule on the road to begin the season, and since we had lost many outstanding players from our previous team, we had many new players who would have to learn the system. Coach Edwards and his staff had cautioned us to be patient with the newer players and told us that we would build confidence as the season progressed.

What I hadn't really anticipated was how much growing *I* would experience in doing my part to see that we came together as a championship-caliber team. And the first three games taught me quite a few lessons—in humility, in working through frustrations, in being a marked man by the defenses, and in teaching the newer players their assignments.

THE DISNEYLAND PIGSKIN CLASSIC

Following a heavy preseason workout schedule, we flew to California to play Florida State University, the number-one-ranked team in the preseason national polls. We had great respect for their program, and we knew that their team had a good chance of winning it all at the end of the season.

We enjoyed the festivities leading up to the game, but when it came time for the kickoff, I was worried. We had made a lot of progress in the previous weeks, but with many of the players having had little or no experience playing on this level, I knew it would be an uphill battle all the way.

Early in the game, when our offense had been forced to give up the ball, I got pretty carried away with my emotions. When we came off the field, I really expressed my anger and frustration in an over-enthusiastic way. I guess the crowd could see this, and even hear it, because after the game, Kim's dad came up to me and asked what I had said. I told him it wasn't very nice. He said, "I know that, but what did you say?" I just laughed and said, "Oh, they were just 'flood in the basement' words."

Getting back to the game, even though Micah Matsuzaki caught four passes for seventy-three yards and was having a great day, we fell behind 28-7 early in the second quarter and couldn't recover. Even though Peter Tuipulotu had two touchdown runs for us, and Erik Hughes caught two touchdown passes in the fourth quarter, Florida State won by a score of 44-28. It was a long day, since they had the ball for almost twice as long as we did; but we learned, and headed back to Provo for a week of school and practicing before returning to L.A. to play UCLA.

UCLA IN THE ROSE BOWL

Playing against Coach Terry Donahue's UCLA Bruins was a second frustrating, learning experience. Although we were down 20-10 by halftime, the momentum changed in our direction during the second half when Ervin Lee intercepted a pass thrown by their quarterback, Tommy Maddox. Two plays later I found Bryce Doman for a nineteen-yard scoring stike, and we pulled to within three at 20-17.

Later in the third quarter, we really thought we had them when Eric Drage pulled in a two-yard scoring toss to put us ahead 23-20. The game wasn't over, though, and they scored on a one-yard run early in the fourth quarter. We had two fourth-quarter drives ourselves, but they both stalled on fourth-down plays. So they beat us 27-23, making us 0-2 for the season.

PENN STATE AT BEAVER STADIUM

We knew the UCLA game had been within our grasp, and it was our own mistakes that cost us the game. But we also knew we were still very young and inexperienced, and we looked forward to a two-week preparation before playing Joe Paterno's fifth-ranked Penn State team.

The week prior to our playing them, the Nittany Lions were jarred by losing to USC; so when our team came to town, they were out to prove something, in a stadium that set a record attendance of 96,304 fans.

Penn State scored first on a thirty-eight-yard field goal, and then on a twelve-yard scoring strike from their quarterback, Tony Sacca, to Terry Smith. But we came back on our own scoring drive, and I was able to toss a seventy-one-yard touchdown pass to Bryce Doman—who broke his collarbone on the same play.

We were still playing well, until we fumbled away the kickoff early in the third quarter. Six plays later they scored, which really took the wind out of our sails. They scored two more touchdowns after that, while holding our offense, and when the final gun sounded, they had beaten us 33-7.

I had felt a lot of pressure, both from the media as well as from the three great defenses we had played, but I had also never known what it was like to start the season with an 0-3 record. It hurt, and I looked forward to getting back to Provo and playing Air Force in the WAC opener.

AIR FORCE—ON OUR TURF

Though thirty thousand less fans showed up in Provo than in Pennsylvania, still our sixty-six thousand fans came to help us get back in the win column, and it felt good. Counting the previous season's losses to Hawaii and Texas A&M, we were 0-5 in the last five games we'd played, and I was never so anxious for a win. However, Air Force was unbeaten in the season, so we knew we were in for a battle.

Even though I had averaged just 217 yards passing in the first three games, some of our positions were beginning to jell, and when the game ended, I had completed twenty of thirty passes for 340 yards and two touchdowns. We had 529 yards in total offense, against their 280 yards, so we felt as if we were starting a new season. We won the game 21-7, with their only score coming in the final three minutes of the game.

UTAH STATE—A NIGHT GAME IN PROVO

The following week found us ready to play the Utah State Aggies, and several of our key players turned in great performances. Our running attack continued to improve, with a 256-yard output. Freshman Mark Atuaia gained ninety-four of these yards on eleven carries, and senior Peter Tuipulotu got sixty-three yards on thirteen carries. He also had nine catches for 184 yards.

Again our defense showed improvement, holding Utah State scoreless until late in the fourth quarter. The final score was 38-10 in our favor. We were on a roll of two wins (which at the time seemed like a *big* roll), and we looked forward to another game in Cougar Stadium the following Saturday.

UNIVERSITY OF TEXAS-EL PASO

Just when we thought things were beginning to go our way, we found ourselves down 10-0, and then 17-7, against UTEP. Needless to say, they were playing extremely well. But then we caught fire, and pulled ahead 28-17 midway through the third quarter. Paul Pitts, a sub for the injured Tony Crutchfield, knocked down a pass for a two-point conversion attempt, which helped.

The game was far from over, though, as they threw an eighty-one-yard touchdown strike and pulled to within two points at 31-29, with less than three minutes remaining.

One of the strangest plays I've ever seen happened next. Their kicker, Ansel Littlejohn, tried an onside kick, and the ball spiralled backwards to their twenty-one-yard line. We thought we had it made about then, but then we fumbled and they got in a position to win the game if they could hit a forty-five-yard field goal attempt by Jason Gillespie. Only fourteen seconds remained in the game when the ball was snapped. But it was snapped high, and our linebacker Scott Giles jumped at just the right time to block the field goal attempt.

Scott was a hero that day, and we preserved the win

to keep our "new season" at 3-0. If we included the "old" part of the season, we were 3-3. It had taken a long time to just get to the break-even point, but we were 2-0 in the WAC, and it felt good.

HAWAII—IN PROVO FOR A CHANGE

It wasn't hard to get up for our next game. It was with the Rainbows, and because of what they had done to us the previous two years in Honolulu, we were eager to play. It was their first trip to Provo in nine years, and we wanted a win—even though we were more concerned about playing to our growing potential, rather than about getting revenge. At least that's what Coach Edwards told us to say.

Anyway, the game started, and I was able to toss a twenty-one-yard scoring strike to Nati Valdez on the opening drive. From there we never looked back. They then fumbled on our two-yard line, and we marched ninety-eight yards in fourteen plays, scoring when I found Matt Zundel in the back of the end zone.

They narrowed the score twice in the second quarter on a touchdown and a field goal, but I pitched the ball out to our great freshman from Las Vegas, Jamal Willis, and we went into the locker room at halftime leading 21-10.

Hawaii fumbled on the first play of the second half, and three plays later I found Eric Drage in the end zone. Our defense then forced them to punt, and we got the ball on our one-yard line. We then engineered a five-play, ninety-nine-yard drive that took just one minute, with Jamal Willis going the final forty-four yards. He was having a career freshman day, and we were all happy for him. We ended up winning our third WAC contest 35-18, and now found ourselves with a winning record at 4-3.

NEW MEXICO IN ALBUQUERQUE

We went to New Mexico to play the Lobos without Peter Tuipulotu, who was out with a bruised thigh. This was a heavy loss for us, but we relied on Mark Atuaia and Jamal Willis, and they combined for 216 of the 263 yards rushing we got for the game.

I had not felt well since when we were flying to Albuquerque, but at the time I dismissed it as air sickness. But later when we got out onto the field, I became violently ill. Even though I was ill throughout the game, our receivers were playing well. As a result, I was able to pass for 375 yards and four touchdowns—to Byron Rex, Eric Mortensen, Itula Mili, and Tyler Anderson. Eric Drage had a career day with nine passes for 230 yards. His efforts were the sixth best of any receiver in BYU's history, and so he had a pretty big smile when we boarded the plane for Salt Lake City. We were now 5-3, with an unblemished 4-0 in the WAC. We had to play Colorado State the following week in Ft. Collins, which would be televised on ESPN. As for me, I couldn't wait for Monday's practice. I knew we were on our way and were really coming together as a unit.

COLORADO STATE—ANOTHER NIGHT GAME

Coach Edwards has never liked to play night games, but I love to play anytime. Even so, when we played Colorado State in a night game, I was still feeling kind of ill from the week before. The players rallied, though, and by the time I was pulled I had connected on twenty-three of twenty-eight passes for 337 yards and three touchdowns. My passing efficiency for the evening was 216, which made me feel about the way Eric had felt the week before. In the Colorado State game, Eric caught three touchdown passes in the first half, so he had another great night.

We won that game 40-17, and found ourselves still on top in the WAC with a 5-0 conference record. We had won six games in a row, and we looked forward to playing the University of Wyoming Cowboys the following week in front of our sixty-six thousand screaming fans. I knew that I wouldn't get to hear them very many more times, so I was going to enjoy it.

The first quarter of the game with Wyoming started slowly for us, and when it ended we were tied 7-7. But from then on it was Jamal Willis and a bunch of great receivers. We scored twenty-four points in the next two quarters, and at one point led 49-10. Jamal had carried for 121 yards, and four of our eight receivers got fifty-plus yards each. The defense even got into the scoring: Jared Leavitt recovered a badly snapped ball on a shotgun-formation play, landing on the ball in the end zone. We out-rushed the Cowboys on the ground 244 yards to 57 yards, and the final score was 56-31 in our favor.

SAN DIEGO STATE—A BIG SURPRISE

We next flew down to San Diego State to play again in Jack Murphy Stadium. It had been a long year since Texas A&M had beaten us there in the Holiday Bowl, and I was eager for us to do well.

What we didn't anticipate as we entered the game was how well San Diego State had mentally prepared for the game with *us*. They were now a contender, and were really looking forward to winning the WAC and then playing in their own stadium for the Holiday Bowl.

The game began, and what happened next became a literal nightmare. We made mistakes that really cost us, and because two of our defensive backs had been suspended from the team that week due to some personal problems they were having, we were not prepared for the home-run bombs San Diego State's quarterback, David Lowery, threw. We had known he might throw a few long bombs, but during the game he just couldn't miss.

Adding to our defensive problems was the gash I received early in the game when I collided face mask to face mask with one of their defenders. It took twenty stitches to close this gash above my left eye, and by then I knew we were in for a battle for the conference championship.

Well into the third quarter we found ourselves down by twenty-eight points. They knew they had us and would win the WAC; but all I could think of was BYU's "Miracle Bowl" in 1980 against Southern Methodist University. With only about four minutes left in that game (the score 45-25 in SMU's favor), Jim McMahon had led BYU to a spectacular come-from-behind win, the final score being 46-45. I'll never forget this "Hail Mary" pass in the final three seconds in pulling out the win. Back then BYU had scored twenty-one points in four minutes for the win; and I knew that we had more than a quarter to do something similar.

So we went to work, and finally tied the game 52-52, with thirty seconds remaining. Coach Edwards told us later that he was too old for moral victories. And so instead of going for the two-point conversion, which would have given us the win, he opted for us to tie, since we could then determine our own destiny as WAC champs the following week with a win over Utah.

When the game ended, their quarterback, David Lowery, had completed twenty-six of thirty-nine passes for 547 yards and five TD's. Because our linemen and receivers never gave up, I had completed thirty-one of fifty-four passes for 599 yards and six TD's. It was quite an offensive showing, and a game I'll never forget. I never thought I would be happy to end a game in a tie. Tyler Anderson scored our final touchdown pass, and so they didn't even have to be creative; they just announced: "From Ty to Ty, for a tie!" It sounds silly now, but at the time I was really happy for our team. We had overcome more adversity, both as a team and as players, than Coach Edwards had ever experienced. And I couldn't wait to play the Utes.

THE FINAL SEASON GAME—
AGAINST THE UNIVERSITY OF UTAH

Even though we had taken quite a defensive beating in San Diego, we were eager to redeem ourselves in our final home game of the season. It would be my last game in front of our great Cougar fans, and along with the rest of the seniors, I wanted to go out with a big win against our rivals from Salt Lake City. If we could win, it would be our eighth straight victory, besides the one tie against San Diego State.

A total of 66,003 fans showed up for the game, and although I could see a few red coats in the north end zone, the stadium looked blue and white as we came out of the locker room to begin the game.

As I warmed up for the first offensive series, I thought back to the conversation Coach Chow had related that he had had earlier in the week with Coach Edwards. It made me pretty emotional when I heard about it. During practice, Norm Chow had gone over to Coach Edwards and asked, "Do you realize this is the last practice number 14 will have for us on this field before a game?" Coach Chow said that that was when it really hit Coach Edwards. Then Coach Edwards told him, "I can't say enough about Ty and how he has helped our program."

It was a good feeling, knowing that the coaches appreciated my competitive spirit, and that I had made a contribution to the Cougar football program. What I didn't anticipate, at that time, was that by the end of the first quarter, we would be leading Utah 14-10.

Our defense was ready this time, and they keyed in on Brian Rowley, Utah's receiver from Orem. One of Rowley's defenders, Tony Crutchfield, had a particularly good game, and our entire team felt that we were hitting on all eight cylinders.

The game finally ended with our winning 48-17. Utah had only managed one legitimate scoring drive against our defense all afternoon, and it felt good to have beaten them for my three years as a starter.

We knew by this time that we would be playing the number-seven-ranked Iowa Hawkeyes in the Holiday Bowl, and even though the game was five weeks away, I was looking forward to it.

OTHER ACTIVITIES

Coach Edwards gave us a couple of weeks off before preparing for our bowl game, and many of our team members needed this time to heal from how beat up we were physically. Football is a heavy contact sport, and the season had handed us our share of injuries.

As for me, I had been lucky enough to avoid any further shoulder problems. And although I had taken a few pretty hard hits during the season, still I felt that I was playing as well as I had ever played. I needed the time away from practice, though, to make the trips that had been planned for me.

The most exciting of these trips was on December 7, when I flew to Kings Mills, Ohio, to attend the first-ever ABC Football Awards show in the College Football Hall of Fame Center. Several awards were announced at that time, and I was excited to hear that I had won the Davey O'Brien Award as the top quarterback in the country. My friend Casey Weldon from Florida State received the Johnny Unitas Golden Arm Award, and I was happy for him. I was also happy for Michigan's Desmond Howard, who won the Maxwell Award as college football's top player. I had gotten that award the year before, and I was happy that he could enjoy it this year.

I was also happy to have been named to the All-America teams again, and to have the various organizations recognize how far our team had progressed during the season. It is a real statement for our administration, coaches, and players that we could come back after the rough start we had.

When I won UPI's Back of the Year the next week, Jeff Shain, the UPI sportswriter, quoted me as saying: "I think this year has been a lot more enjoyable, gratifying year. To start off 0-3 and come back to finish 8-3-1, we feel like we've done a great job of making progress.

"We've got a lot of young players, and it's great to see those guys work hard instead of just waiting for the next year. To see them working as hard as they did to get us back on top, that was one of the high points of the year for me.

"For me, personally, throwing for fifteen thousand yards is something one of my coaches mentioned earlier in the year, saying he'd like to see me shoot for it. I didn't really think I had a chance until we played San Diego State. That's probably the one record that will stick in my mind the most."

In talking about the Heisman race and how Desmond Howard would likely win it, Mr. Shain again quoted me as saying, "I realize the only people I have to please are the coaches and myself. As long as I do that, I'm going to be all right."

That was honestly how I felt, too, and so the next weekend when I was invited, along with Desmond Howard, Casey Weldon, and Washington's All-American defensive lineman, Steve Entman, to participate as a finalist in the Heisman balloting, I really felt honored.

Having won the award the year before, I knew how it could change a person's life, even though not always for the best. And even though I was confident that Desmond would win it, I was excited to be flying back again to New York, this time with Kim as my wife. In a way, that was where things all began for us the year before, and I knew we could just relax this time.

Desmond did win the award, and Kim and I were happy for him and for his family, who watched the ceremonies. I enjoyed being with him and the other finalists, and we had a great vacation again in New York City. Much had happened since our first coming there the year before, so we felt more comfortable this time, and knew where we wanted to go and what we wanted to see.

Following the award ceremonies, we flew directly to Nashville, Tennessee, where Bob Hope was again preparing for his annual Christmas TV special. Because I was a repeat on the Associated Press All-America team, I was invited to again meet with him and to be announced during his Christmas special.

Mr. Hope is a great man, as I had learned in Miami the year before. He has quite a sense of humor, too; and when my name was announced during the taping, he shook my hand and said, "Yeah, Ty was last year's Heisman Trophy winner, and he's back this year as a second-time All-American. Ty, as a passer, is going to be very valuable in the pros, and he knows it. He carries his right arm around in his wallet."

We all laughed, and although I really did hope to make a good living as a professional quarterback, my main goal was to get back to Provo and start throwing in preparation for the Holiday Bowl.

HOLIDAY BOWL '91—BYU VS. IOWA

When I returned to the Y, I had to finish my final papers as well as take my final exams. Kim had the same pressure. So even though the team and I began working out, my mind was pretty much focused on getting through the week of finals.

After this was accomplished, Coach Edwards held a team meeting, and the word for us this year seemed to be *focus*. We knew how good Iowa was, and because we remembered how our being somewhat laid-back in preparing for Texas A&M the previous year had contributed to our losing that game, we were determined not to be caught off guard.

We left for San Diego a full week before the game, and had a great time enjoying the warm, beautiful climate as well as the red-carpet treatment that the city gave to us. But even though these other activities took much of our time, the coaches changed their preparation philosophy and we had four extra practices, including one on Christmas Day. So by Monday night, December 30, we felt that we were ready to play. We had great respect for Coach Hayden Fry and for his team. But we knew we had been set back six weeks earlier, before a national audience on ESPN, in the 52-52 tie with San Diego State. What made it worse was something an Iowa sportswriter wrote before the game. He suggested that BYU stood for "Bring Your Undertaker." They didn't respect our defense, and we wanted to change that image.

But even with all of this buildup, our defense came out and played tentatively. Before we were twelve minutes into the game, we were behind 13-0.

By this time, even though I was quite frustrated, I felt that we could play better, and we did. Our problem, though, was that we just weren't able to punch the ball into the end zone. Several of us made mistakes, and these mistakes seemed to kill us, even though we held Iowa's great offensive attack scoreless for the final forty-three minutes of the game.

We finally scored in the second quarter after a seventy-eight-yard drive of our own. I threw a nine-yard pass to Peter Tuipulotu, and we missed the extra point.

We were only down 13-6 going into the locker room at halftime.

Even though we moved the ball well and controlled the game from this point on, we could score on only two of our six drives inside their twenty-yard line. Our final touchdown came in the fourth quarter on a twenty-nine-yard pass to Tyler Anderson in a fourth-and-four situation. He did a great job catching the ball in the end zone, and because there was still plenty of time left, we kicked the ball for a sure tie.

On the final drive of the game, we moved the ball all the way down the field. I was feeling great. It was first-and-ten on Iowa's eighteen-yard line, and we had twenty-six seconds to play. It was a sure win with a field goal, but I thought we could go for it and beat them as soundly as we had played.

I received the snap, rolled around to the left, and rifled the ball to Byron Rex, our tight end. But the throw came a little fast and was high, so it sailed through his hands without his catching it. This wouldn't have been so bad, but he deflected it just enough for it to then land right in the arms of Iowa's MVP cornerback, Carlos James.

The game ended, and even though we had out-played the seventh-ranked team in the country, we had been forced to settle for a tie. I should have known better than to throw a pass as I did, but football is a game of crucial plays, and we just didn't come up with that play when we needed it. My philosophy has always been one of living life to its fullest. I want to give it my all. I knew that even though there were risks and possible setbacks, I would only be happy if I played every down as though we were going to score.

I felt good about my own stats, having completed twenty-nine of forty-four passes for 350 yards and two touchdowns. Still, that last interception was a hard one to accept.

One of our fans, a very nice lady, came up to me after I had left the locker room. Her words made me smile when she said, "Ty, you started out with an interception, and you finished with an interception—but we liked everything in between."

This lady's comment was said in fun, and I appreciated her kind words. I knew that our team had played well and that we had redeemed ourselves in the eyes of the country. Our program was strong, and with all of the outstanding players returning for the '92 season, I knew BYU would continue to enjoy the tradition of winning.

While this is a personal thing, I feel that our team's tradition of having a competitive spirit and going all out to win is important to personal growth and development. The lessons of life provided in this unusual environment are too many to mention, but I have enjoyed being part of the outstanding Cougar student/athlete program. I had wanted to make a difference when I had first arrived in Provo, and people were more than kind in reassuring me that I had.

If I never played another down of football, I felt happy that at least to some my priorities were in line, and I had represented the Cougars from BYU in a manner that was equal to who they are.

Living Life with Dignity and Purpose

THE JAPAN BOWL

As my collegiate career drew to a close, Kim and I were invited to Japan, where I was given the opportunity of playing in the annual Japan Bowl. We knew that we would have to limit our postseason playing commitments, since we both had to take a full load of classes in order to graduate. But we also knew that this would be a great experience, and that we could enjoy the cultural exchange and have a good time playing with the other graduating seniors who would be there.

After we had accepted this invitation, I was informed that I was named a recipient of the NCAA's annual award called Today's Top Six. This award was meant to honor the year's top six athletes in all sports within the NCAA. While 50 percent of the award was based on athletic achievement, 25 percent was based on academic achievement, and 25 percent was based on character, leadership, and community service.

Prior to my receiving this award, six former Cougar athletes had received it. They were as follows: Terry Sanford, quarterback, 1971; Gifford Nielsen, quarterback,

1978; Marc Wilson, quarterback, 1980; Steve Young, quarterback, 1984; Ed Eyestone, track, 1986; and Dylann Duncan, women's volleyball, 1989. I felt very honored to have been included in this company, and we found out that in all of the NCAA, only USC had produced more Top Six winners than BYU.

But we had a problem in that the award was to be given on Wednesday evening, January 8—which was right in the middle of the week that we would be in Japan.

Kim and I felt that we needed to be in attendance; so after spending several days in Japan, preparing to play the game and being hosted by the Japanese people, we flew back to Los Angeles for the awards ceremony.

Coach Glen Tuckett, our athletic director, came down to L.A. and was with us for the occasion.

In the *Today's Top Six* program, they stated the following:

Ty Detmer—The recipient of the 1990 Heisman Trophy, inducted as college football's outstanding player, Detmer has enjoyed a record-breaking career as quarterback of the Brigham Young football team. The first Brigham Young player to be elected captain as a sophomore, he has broken 62 NCAA records and tied four more, while winning two consecutive Davey O'Brien Awards (1990 and 1991) as the nation's outstanding quarterback. A three-time All-America selection (1989, 1990, 1991), his most outstanding campaign was 1990, when, in addition to earning the Heisman, he was awarded the Maxwell Trophy, and was named the United Press International player of the year.

Spokesperon for Brigham Young's Earth Science Museum, Detmer has compiled a 2.630 grade-point average, while majoring in recreation management. A United Way volunteer, he is heavily involved in community activities in the Provo, Utah, area. He speaks regularly to civic, youth and business organizations, participates in local cancer crusades, teaches 8-year-olds in a local Mormon church, and has taped several drug-awareness promotions.

I was especially grateful that they had mentioned the community service activities I had been involved in, as well as my calling in the Church. It felt good to be recognized for involvement in worthwhile activities independent of athletics, and Kim and I felt happy that we had made the effort to attend the ceremonies with the other five recipients.

Following this evening of recognition, we stayed the night in Los Angeles and then flew right back to Japan.

When we arrived in Tokyo, the Latter-day Saint missionaries met us at the airport. They took us to the mission home of the Japan Tokyo South Mission, and we ate dinner with them and President and Sister William Walker. They then escorted us to the Tokyo Stake Center to a Church fireside for all of the Tokyo stakes and missions. In addition, members and nonmembers in the military attended, bringing the numbers to about six hundred people in the congregation.

Brian May, who served a mission to Japan, spoke first, after which I shared my thoughts. Brother Makoto Oki was my translator, and in all the talks I have given, this was the first time I had attempted to speak with a translator. Sharing my thoughts about joining the Church, about my family and Kim's family, as well as my excitement about preparing for a temple marriage in a few weeks to my beautiful wife, Kim, was especially rewarding. I also expressed my testimony of the Savior, and it was an evening we will always remember.

The Japanese are very polite people, much like Texans, and we were honored to spend the evening with them, even though we were tired from the jet lag.

Before leaving the fireside, we went into another room where I was able to throw a football to about twenty-five young boys, who had looked forward to that experience. We then signed autographs for about a half hour, took pictures, and visited. The Japan Bowl committee had sent a photographer to the fireside, and the missionaries were able to meet him and give him a copy of the Book of Mormon.

We then left, and literally collapsed in our room at the Takanawa Prince Hotel.

The following day we did some sight-seeing and then held a final practice. Finally, after quite a week of activities—and after having traveled from Utah to Japan, then back to Los Angeles, then back to Japan—we played the game. I'm not sure if my legs and head were ready to play, but I warmed up, and soon the game was under way.

After both teams got off to a slow start, we connected on a couple of passes, and then Joe Wood of Air Force kicked a field goal for us. Not long after that we moved the ball down again, and he scored a second field goal. This put us ahead 6-0 at the half. I played the first and third quarters, with Iowa's Matt Rodgers quarterbacking our team the second and fourth quarters. It felt different having our Holiday Bowl opponent's quarterback sharing time with me on the same team, but I respected him as a person and a player and for being named to the All-Big Ten team two years running.

This sharing of quarterback duties meant that I could go out in the second half and really get us going.

The second half finally started, and sure enough, we moved the ball eighty-nine yards in twelve plays, completing passes of fifteen, eighteen, and five yards, and scrambling for twenty-three yards. The coaches then called a quarterback draw from the four-yard line; and so I backed up, then ran forward and lunged uncontested into the end zone. The players wanted to dance in the end zone, doing what they call "ride the horse." So we did that, and all celebrated. After making the extra point, we were ahead 13-0.

But the East team put together two scoring drives in the fourth quarter, and even though our West team made a valiant effort, the East won 14-13.

Following the game, the officials made three award

presentations. Two members of the East team received the offensive and defensive MVP awards, and I was fortunate to receive the Joe Roth Memorial Award. This award was given to the most inspirational player in the game, and I was glad to have made that impression.

Kim and I enjoyed getting to know the other players and coaches, and even though we didn't pull off the victory, the trip (and in Kim's and my case, the *two* trips) and the experiences we had were worthwhile, and we were glad we went. It was an enjoyable way to end my collegiate career.

MY PHILOSOPHY OF LIFE

As I've thought about my life and what motivates me to do the things I do, I have found that there have been at least seven underlying values present in my life. I'm sure there are many others, but for now I would like to share the following, which I have called my "Keys for Success."

Key Number One. Not long ago a friend asked me what my philosophy of life is. Without really thinking I blurted, "Hunting." He was as surprised at my response as I think I was. But when I thought about it more, I realized that *spending time doing what I enjoy doing* really is one of my basic priorities.

For me, other than spending time with Kim (or better yet, taking her with me), the thing I enjoy doing most is getting out in the mountains, hunting. I love nature, and being up in the pines and quakies and breathing that fresh mountain air is like being in heaven. In addition to participating in the sport of responsibly thinning the wildlife herds, I can unwind out there, and clearing my mind in that way gives me renewed strength to then go back and face whatever challenges I may have at the time.

Closely related to this is my belief that we should choose a profession that we love. I have been told that most adults in America work at jobs they don't enjoy. They have a need to survive, and once they get locked into a routine, they just resign themselves to "gutting it out" until they retire.

As folks would think, I hope to spend my life in athletics—first as a professional football player, then as a coach. I love the game—not only for the high of winning, but more important for the experience of *playing*. Learning to win graciously, to lose without despair, to turn the skill level up a notch, to meet the challenges of a coming game—all of these things are exciting to me. These experiences, and many more, are lessons that I would like to continue learning, and then pass on to young men of the next generation.

Athletics can bring out the best and the worst in us, and I think that my dad has the greatest teaching techniques that a coach can have in building young men—not just in winning games. I also think this is why coaches around the country have such high respect for Coach Edwards. His life is not spent in winning games, although that comes with it; but his life is spent in building men who can then leave the university setting and contribute positively to society.

But in the end, a profession should be *fun*. As my dad always said, leave it when it is no longer fun. Hopefully, for me and athletics, that will not be for a long, long time.

Key Number Two. The second key for me in being successful is to *learn how to compete successfully*. That doesn't mean learning to be better than other players or other people. But it does mean developing a competitor's mentality—not spending all of one's leisure hours sitting in front of a TV.

I think a lot of parents are afraid to have their sons

and daughters enter into organized sports, regardless of which sport it might be. They don't want their children learning negative behavior; or even worse, getting hurt.

These concerns are valid, too. But as I look back on when I began—in first grade playing tee-ball—I saw more kids getting hurt playing on their bikes in the neighborhood than I did in actual controlled team competition. And, too, if parents are selective about the league, the coaches, and so forth, they can involve their children in a healthy environment that really develops self-esteem.

Growing up playing organized sports taught me so many lessons. I learned dedication, work ethics, goal setting, teamwork, unselfishness; I learned how to respond to adversity, how to win and how to lose, how to develop a winning mentality—all of these things, and more.

I will always be grateful to my dad and to Paw Paw for stressing this form of competition—striving to be better in the next season than I had been in the previous one. And I will never be able to repay my mom for the literally hundreds of practices and games she took me to. Even though she had many things to do with her time, she would never be too tired to take me where I had to go. Folks always give my dad credit for my being competitive, and I know that he did a lot towards this. But behind the scenes, without fanfare, my mom is one of the most competitive people I know.

Kim's folks have shared this same commitment to their kids, and I admire them for that. I just hope Kim and I can be the kind of parents that we both have—for they have seen the good that comes from healthy competition. I think we're better people for it.

Key Number Three. Another key to success I have discovered is *learning to face adversity and to lose*. From what I've seen, no one goes through life without having problems, thereby being forced to learn to lose. No one, including me, likes to learn what it's like to face this type of adversity. But it's part of life, and something we must all experience.

From what I've learned, the important thing is to be able to rebound from a loss—to learn what lessons are there to be learned, then to get back up and start all over again, with an even greater perspective than we had before we had a particular setback.

If I had taken my first BYU game against Wyoming and allowed those four interceptions to tell me that I wasn't good enough to play on the major college level, I would have missed out on some of the greatest moments of my life. It would have been quite easy that weekend to just fly back to Texas and go fishing. But I've always been grateful that I had coaches and older players who put their arms around me, helped dust me off, and then encouraged me to get ready for a win the next week. It was a great lesson to internalize at that embarrassing and confidence-shattering moment.

Key Number Four. "Tying" the last two games of my senior season was one of the greatest, and most unexpected, growing experiences for me. And each of the ties brought such different emotions. I had great feelings about the first one against San Diego State, because we had done almost the impossible by coming from so far behind. But the second tie against Iowa in the Holiday Bowl was the result of our entire team, including me, making crucial mistakes, and that tie *hurt*. Iowa didn't beat us, and they didn't even tie us. We tied *them* because we didn't perform to our potential during the crucial moments of the game.

Someone once said that being average is being as near the bottom as the top. A tie doesn't necessarily mean we're average, but the important thing is that we play up to our potential—whether in an athletic contest or in the game of life.

So after this lengthy introduction, my fourth key to

success is *developing a goal-setting mentality, and then playing and living up to our personal potential.* There will always be someone better, as well as someone worse, than each of us. But when we learn to compare ourselves *with ourselves,* regardless of the outcome of a given event, then we have learned an invaluable lesson of life.

Key Number Five. One of the greatest discoveries a person can make, at least from my experience, is *learning to find balance.* This fifth key to success is actually quite rare, and in a way is woven into the other six keys. Most people, including a lot of athletes, pride themselves in "eating, drinking, and sleeping" whatever they are into. My dad always encouraged Koy and me, as well as Dee and Lori, to get involved in as many sports and activities as we could. Maybe this is why I enjoy a good round of golf or an early-morning hour of fishing every bit as much as I enjoy a high-intensity football game. Each of these experiences brings out different emotions, and each is as satisfying as the others.

As I have tried to portray throughout this book, everyone, including myself, has his or her weaknesses and strengths. But I have tried to put these weaknesses in perspective and grow from them rather than just ignore them. An example of this is my different aptitude toward various college courses. Like most others, I have taken them all, and have done better in some than in others. But the point is, I *went* to college, I kept my body and mind free from harmful substances, and this education has now become a significant part of my identity.

Part of college life, whether in the classroom or out on the practice and playing field, is the opportunity of learning to work. I have associated with several gifted athletes who never performed to their full potential. Some of my best friends are in this category, and I feel bad for them because they aren't as happy or as productive as they otherwise might have been.

My wife, Kim, as well as my former roommate Eric Mortensen have been two of the people—other than my parents and family—who have helped me understand the need for spiritual values. At the present time, Kim and I are co-teachers in our ward's Primary organization, and one of our greatest thrills is preparing a lesson each week, then going to church and teaching those eight-year-old kids a facet of the gospel. Again, it's a matter of balance, and I wouldn't want to live my life without it.

Key Number Six. Throughout my life I have had good role models and bad ones. Those who have been a positive influence are those who have *been* what they said they were and have *done* what they said they would do. These people, then, have *learned to be individuals of integrity*.

My parents and grandparents have always said that we need to be people who are taken for our word. I know that a man's reputation is the most important thing about him, and I will always be thankful for growing up in a home where that was stressed.

As I have mentioned, following the Heisman win during my junior year of eligibility, the press asked me again and again if I was going to change my mind and leave college so that I could get a nice professional contract. I wasn't trying to be a hero or anything when I said that I would do what I had told Coach Edwards I would do five years earlier, when I told him I was coming to BYU.

I think that for quarterbacks, maybe more so than for other players, a university and its team have to be able to count on a commitment that is made. For me, it wasn't really an issue of what I would or would not do. I had committed to play through my senior year of eligibility; that's what I had told Coach Edwards I would do. So the decision had already been made. To keep commitments is what I have been taught, and doing so illustrates what I think is maybe the most important element of success out of the six I have named.

Key Number Seven. I don't plan on leaving this earth for a long, long time. But when I do, I hope it can be said of me that I was someone who learned how to think of others. *Learning to be a charitable person*, then, is the final ingredient in my formula.

As I have gone through my college years, a lot of attention has come my way. This has been embarrassing for me at times; but it has also been fun. But there have been costs, too. One week when the team wins, everyone thinks I'm doing a great job, and then next week when we lose, the loss is also mine to shoulder.

I'll admit that there have been times when a loss has been my fault, and I've accepted the responsibility. But one thing that I have tried to be, whether we have played well enough to win or not, is someone who *cared*.

Not long ago, Kim and I were driving down the street. We saw a young man sitting in a wheelchair out near the curb. He was all decked out in a BYU football jersey and so forth, and we could tell that he was a Cougar fan. So about then Kim looks over at me and says, "Ty, I think we should go back there and visit with that boy. It would really make him happy."

In a way, I was surprised by Kim's invitation, because we were in a hurry to go somewhere. But in another way, I wasn't surprised at all. She is that kind of example to me.

So I turned the car around, drove back to where the boy was sitting, and we both got out of the car and had a brief but enjoyable visit. Again, I wasn't a hero to do this—but Kim *was* a hero, in my eyes, and I'll always remember the feeling of our making the day happier for that crippled young man. He doesn't have the same opportunities in life that Kim and I do, and yet he's totally into life and living! I learned more from Kim, and from that young man, than they learned from me.

We can either become someone who reads his or her own press clippings, or become someone who tries to reach out to others, even when it's not convenient. My mom and dad always taught me to treat other people the way I wanted to be treated. My dad can be at a coaches' convention, with all the other coaches milling around visiting, and he will leave those coaches and go over and spend time with the custodian. He'll talk to him about deer hunting or whatever the man wants to talk about. From where I stand, this is what being called a Christian is all about. And as far as I am concerned, this is the thing that matters most.

To summarize, then, let me restate my formula for meeting life's challenges:

Keys for Success

Number One: Spend time doing what you enjoy
Number Two: Learn how to compete successfully
Number Three: Learn to face adversity and to lose
Number Four: Develop a goal-setting mentality, then live up to your potential
Number Five: Learn to find balance
Number Six: Be a person of integrity
Number Seven: Be a quietly caring Christian

An End and a Beginning

BECOMING AN ELDER IN THE CHURCH

On Super Bowl Sunday, January 26, 1992, the Herbert family came down to spend the day with Kim and me and to attend church with us in the Pleasant Grove Fourteenth Ward. Kim and I were both pretty excited about this day, because I had been found worthy to receive the Melchizedek Priesthood and to be ordained to the office of an elder in that priesthood.

Following our sacrament services, we all met in the high council room. There, under the direction of the high councilor in charge, I did receive this priesthood. Kim's dad bestowed it on me, and gave me a nice blessing. Assisting him in the circle were family members as well as ward priesthood leaders, and I appreciated their support.

After my ordination, we left the church and drove over to our home. We then ate dinner as a family and played games while we watched the Super Bowl.

BEING SEALED IN THE SALT LAKE TEMPLE

February 6, 1991, the day of my baptism, was one of the most important days of my life. It had this importance because it laid the foundation for the events that took place one year and a day later.

Kim wants to share her thoughts here, and since this will probably be the only time that I get the last word, I'll let her do that:

"For the past four years of my life since meeting this shy, quiet boy from Texas, I have known happiness. Ty can tease with the best of them and is never without a smile on his face—but he is also the most genuine and caring person I know. We both had the same strict guidelines, in terms of our values and goals, but in our relationship he was always the leader. With Ty, there is no halfway. It is all the way, and then some.

"I have never known a time that Ty has put his own interests or needs ahead of others. They will come first, no matter what. I'll give his parents and grandparents the credit for his being this way, and from where I stand at his side, this is what makes him stand so tall. He especially loves kids, and wherever we go he always seeks them out of the crowd and spends time with them. This is going to make it challenging for me as we begin our family; I want to be as good with children as Ty is. But my mother was a great example to me, in terms of what a mother should be, so I look forward to the day our first child is born with as much anticipation as Ty does. He is not just great when he is in public. But in the quiet of our lives, when it is just the two of us, he is the greatest husband a woman could have."

Kim said more than I had expected, so I'll now get the last word in.

Since I have known her, Kim has always been an example to me as a strong person. If something wasn't right, she would always stand up for her beliefs and do what she could to make it right.

Kim has also been a lot of fun to be with. She is a happy person and always upbeat. I always said that I would marry someone who is happy, because then I'd be happy. First she was my friend, then my *best* friend. And now she is my wife, the woman I have chosen to spend my life and my eternities with.

On the morning of February 7, 1992, Kim and I, along with family and close friends, journeyed to the Salt Lake Temple. President Thomas S. Monson greeted us and those who were there to enjoy this special event.

After President Monson performed the sealing ceremony, as we were outside taking pictures, Kim and I reflected on the hour we had just spent inside the temple. We knew that with the way our love for each other was growing, if we would just live right, we would one day, along with our families, be together forever.

I felt that this was a special moment in my life—a destination I had reached after years of preparation. But since then, the more I've thought about it, the more I realize that for me and for my loved ones this is only a beginning.

Ty Detmer Statistics

NCAA RECORDS
(59 Broken, 3 Tied)

TOTAL OFFENSE (27)

1. Most yards gained, 2 years: 9,455. *(Old record: 8,085, Jim McMahon, BYU, 1980–81.)*
2. Most yards gained, 3 years: 10,644. *(Old record: 9,640, Jim McMahon, BYU, 1978, 1980–81.)*
3. Most yards gained by a sophomore: 4,433. *(Old record: 4,299, Scott Mitchell, Utah, 1988.)*
4. Highest average yards gained per play, career: 8.18. *(Old record: 7.49, Steve Young, BYU, 1981–83.)*
5. Most games gaining 300 yards or more, season: 12. *(Old record: 11, Jim McMahon, BYU, 1980.)*
6. Most games gaining 300 yards or more, career: 33. *(Old record: 18, Steve Young, BYU, 1981–83.)*
7. Most consecutive games gaining 300 yards or more, season: 12. *(Old record: 11, Jim McMahon, BYU, 1980.)*
8. Most consecutive games gaining 300 yards or more, career: 19. *(Old record: 12, Jim McMahon, BYU, 1978–81.)*

9. Most games gaining 400 yards or more, career: 13. *(Old record: 9, Jim McMahon, BYU, 1978–81.)*

10. Most consecutive games gaining 400 yards or more, season: 5. *(Old record: 4, Jim McMahon, BYU, 1980.)*

11. Most consecutive games gaining 400 yards or more, career: 5. *(Old record: 4, Jim McMahon, BYU, 1980.)*

12. Most TD's responsible for, 3 years: 96. *(Old record: 93, Jim McMahon, BYU, 1978, 1980–81.)*

13. Most TD's responsible for, 4 years: 135. *(Old record: 94, Jim McMahon, BYU, 1977–78, 1980–81.)*

14. Most TD's responsible for per game, 3 years: 2.82. *(Old record: 2.81, Jim McMahon, BYU, 1978, 1980–81.)*

15. Most points responsible for, 3 years: 582. *(Old record: 562, Jim McMahon, BYU, 1978, 1980–81.)*

16. Most points responsible for, career: 826. *(Old record: 562, Jim McMahon, BYU, 1977–81.)*

17. Most points responsible for per game, 3 years: 17.1. *(Old record: 17.0, Jim McMahon, BYU, 1978, 1980–81.)*

18. Highest average yards gained per play, season: 8.92. *(Old record: 8.57, Jim McMahon, BYU, 1980.)*

19. Most yards gained, career: 15,031. *(Old record: 11,317, Doug Flutie, Boston College.)*

20. Most yards gained against one opponent (SDSU), career: 1,483. *(Old record: 1,445, Doug Flutie, Boston College, against Penn State.)*

21. Most yards gained per game against one opponent (SDSU), career: 370.8. *(Old record: 361.3, Doug Flutie, Boston College, against Penn State.)*

22. Most seasons gaining 3,000 yards or more: 3. *(Old record: 2, by many players.)*

23. Most plays, 3 years: 1,548. *(Old record: 1,503, Gene Swick, Toledo, 1973–75.)*

24. Most plays, 4 years: 1,795. *(Old record: 1,722, Todd Santos, SDSU, 1984–87.)*

25. Most TD's responsible for per game, career: 2.93. *(Old record: 2.56, Johnny Bright, Drake.)*

26. Most points responsible for per game, career: 17.9. *(Old record: 15.4, Johnny Bright, Drake.)*
27. Most yards gained per game, career: 319.4. *(Old record: 309.1, Mike Perez, San Jose State, 1986–87.)*

TOTAL OFFENSE RECORDS TIED (1)

1. Most seasons gaining 2,500 yards or more: 3. *(Record achieved by six others.)*

PASSING (32)

1. Most passes completed per game, 2 years: 26.1. *(Old record: 25.3, Jim McMahon, BYU, 1980–81.)*
2. Most yards gained, season: 5,188. *(Old record: 4,699, Andre Ware, Houston, 1989.)*
3. Most yards gained, 2 years: 9,748. *(Old record: 8,148, Robbie Bosco, BYU, 1984–85.)*
4. Most yards gained, 3 years: 11,000. *(Old record: 9,433, Jim McMahon, BYU, 1978, 1980–81.)*
5. Most yards gained per game, 2 years: 406.2. *(Old record: 369.4, Jim McMahon, BYU, 1980–81.)*
6. Most yards gained per game, 3 years: 323.5. *(Old record: 303.78, Andre Ware, Houston, 1987–89.)*
7. Most consecutive games gaining 300 yards or more, career 24. *(Old record: 12, Jim McMahon, BYU.)*
8. Most TD passes, 3 years: 86. *(Old record: 83, Jim McMahon, BYU, 1978, 1980–81.)*
9. Most TD passes, career: 121. *(Old record: 84, Jim McMahon, BYU, 1977–81.)*
10. Most consecutive games throwing 1 or more TD passes: 35. *(Old record: 22, Steve Young, BYU, 1982–83.)*
11. Most yards gained by a sophomore: 4,560. *(Old record: 4,322, Scott Mitchell, BYU, 1988.)*
12. Most games gaining 300 yards or more, season: 12 (twice). *(Old record: 11, Jim McMahon, BYU.)*

13. Most consecutive games gaining 300 yards or more, season: 12. *(Old record: 11, Jim McMahon, BYU.)*
14. Most consecutive games gaining 200 yards or more, career: 27. *(Old record: 22, Steve Young, BYU.)*
15. Most games gaining 300 yards or more, career: 33. *(Old record: 17, Jim McMahon, BYU, 1977–81.)*
16. Most games gaining 400 yards or more, career: 12.
17. Most yards gained per pass attempt (min. 237 atts.), season: 11.07 (412 for 4,560). *(Old record: 10.27, Jim McMahon, BYU, 1980.)*
18. Most yards gained per completion (min. 205 comps.), season: 17.21 (265 for 4,560). *(Old record: 16.10, Jim McMahon, BYU, 1980.)*
19. Most TD passes, freshman and sophomore seasons: 45 (13 and 32). *(Old record: 40 [15 and 25], Bernie Kosar, Miami [Fla.], 1983.)*
20. Most yards gained per pass attempt, career: 9.82 (1,530 for 15,031). *(Old record: 9.00, Jim McMahon, BYU, 1977–81.)*
21. Most TD passes at conclusion of junior year: 86.
22. Most yards gained, career: 15,031. *(Old record: 11,425, Todd Santos, SDSU, 1984–87.)*
23. Most games gaining 200 yards or more, career: 38. *(Old record: 30, Kevin Sweeney, Brian McClure, Doug Flutie.)*
24. Most yards gained against one opponent (N. Mexico), career: 1,495. *(Old record: 1,482, Doug Flutie, Boston College, against Penn State.)*
25. Most yards gained per game against one opponent (N. Mexico), career: 373.8. *(Old record: 370.5, Doug Flutie, Boston College, against Penn State.)*
26. Most passes completed, 3 years: 875. *(Old record: 787, Brian McClure, Bowling Green.)*
27. Most passes attempted, 3 years: 1,377. *(Old record: 1,251, Brian McClure, Bowling Green.)*
28. Most passes attempted, 4 years: 1,530. *(Old record: 1,484, Todd Santos, SDSU, 1984–87.)*

29. Most passes completed, 4 years: 958. *(Old record: 910, Todd Santos, SDSU, 1984–87.)*
30. Most yards gained per game, career: 326.8. *(Old record: 309.7, Mike Perez, San Jose State, 1986–87.)*
31. Most yards gained per completion, career: 15.68. *(Old record: 15.62, Doug Flutie, Boston College, 1981–84.)*
32. Highest passing efficiency, career: 162.7. *(Old record: 156.9, Jim McMahon, BYU, 1977–81.)*

PASSING RECORDS TIED (2)

1. Most consecutive games gaining 200 yards or more, season: 12 (twice). *(Ties Robbie Bosco, BYU, 1984 and 1985.)*
2. Most games gaining 200 yards or more, season: 12 (twice). *(Ties Robbie Bosco, BYU, 1984 and 1985.)*

HONORS

1991

Team Captain

Davey O'Brien Award

Third in the Heisman Trophy Balloting

First Team All-America, Kodak (Coaches)

First Team All-America, Football Writers

First Team All-America, Associated Press

First Team All-America, United Press International

First Team All-America, *Sporting News*

First Team All-America, *College and Pro Football Newsweekly*

Third Team All-America, *Football News*

UPI Back of the Year

Western Athletic Conference Offensive Player of the Year

First Team All-WAC

WAC Offensive Player of the Week (Oct. 31)

Co-WAC Offensive Player of the Week (Nov. 16)

Sports Illustrated Offensive Player of the Week (Nov. 16)

Toyota Leadership Award (San Diego St.)

AT&T Long-Distance Award (Utah)

Today's Top Six Award, NCAA

Japan Bowl

Athlete of the Year, *Deseret News*

1990

Team Captain

Heisman Trophy Winner

Maxwell Trophy Winner

Davey O'Brien Award

The Victor Award, City of Hope
  College Athlete of the Year

First Team All-America, AP

First Team All-America, UPI

First Team All-America,
  Football Writers

First Team All-America,
  Walter Camp

First Team All-America,
  Football News

First Team All-America,
  Sporting News

UPI Player of the Year

CBS Player of the Year

Football News
  Player of the Year

First Team All-America,
  Scripps Howard

Scripps Howard
  Player of the Year

WAC Player of the Year

First-Team All-Wac,
  Unanimous

WAC Offensive
  Player of the Week (Miami)

CNN Player of the Week
  (Miami)

Football News
  Player of the Week (Miami)

Athlon Player of the Week
  (Miami)

WAC Offensive Player
  of the Week (San Diego St.)

Chevrolet Player of the Game
  (San Diego St.)

CBS Toyota Leadership Award
  (San Diego St.)

WAC Offensive Player
  of the Week (Air Force)

Amateur Athlete of the Year,
  U.S. Sports Academy
  (Alabama)

Amateur Athlete of September,
  U.S. Sports Academy
  (Alabama)

Athlete of the Month for
  September, *Deseret News*

Athlete of the Year,
  Deseret News

1989

Team Captain

First Team All-WAC, Coaches

First Team All-WAC, Media

Honorable Mention
  All-America, UPI

Honorable Mention All-America,
  Sporting News

CNN Player of the Week
  (San Diego St.)

WAC Offensive Player
  of the Week (UTEP)

Chevrolet Player of the Game
  (Air Force)

COLLEGE RECORD GAME-BY-GAME

1988 Opponent	RUSHING					PASSING						Plays	TO	S
	Carries	Gain	Loss	Net	TD	Att.	Comp.	Int.	Yards	TD	%			
Wyoming	6	7	46	-39	0	26	9	4	133	1	.346	32	94	5
Texas	0	0	0	0	0	3	2	0	64	1	.667	3	64	0
UTEP	4	0	13	-13	0	14	8	0	82	1	.571	18	69	1
Utah St.	2	5	5	0	0	5	3	0	13	0	.600	7	13	0
Colorado St.	0	0	0	0	0	0	0	0	0	0	.000	0	0	0
TCU	Did not play													
Hawaii	1	0	4	-4	0	10	5	0	132	1	.500	11	128	0
New Mexico	5	13	24	-11	0	35	24	0	333	5	.686	40	322	2
San Diego St.	7	27	14	13	0	13	6	1	45	0	.462	20	58	2
Air Force	Did not play													
Utah	2	32	5	27	0	20	10	2	238	2	.500	22	265	1
Miami	5	3	19	-16	0	27	16	3	212	2	.593	32	196	3
*Colorado	4	4	14	-10	0	17	11	0	129	1	.647	21	119	1
Totals: (Pass Efficiency: 138.0)	32	87	130	-43	0	153	83	10	1,252	13	.542	185	1,209	14

1989 Opponent	RUSHING					PASSING						Plays	TO	S
	Carries	Gain	Loss	Net	TD	Att.	Comp.	Int.	Yards	TD	%			
New Mexico	11	35	56	-21	1	29	19	0	323	0	.655	40	302	4
Wash. St.	10	59	34	25	0	53	34	3	537	4	.642	63	562	5
Navy	2	6	5	1	0	35	26	0	353	2	.743	37	354	0
Utah St.	6	24	12	12	0	35	18	2	330	3	.514	41	342	2
Wyoming	10	6	55	-49	0	30	16	0	337	2	.533	40	288	6
Colorado St.	7	11	27	-16	1	38	20	2	338	3	.526	45	322	3
UTEP	4	9	12	-3	1	28	22	2	426	3	.786	32	423	0
Hawaii	13	12	89	-77	0	35	24	2	427	1	.686	48	350	10
Oregon	11	37	45	-8	0	47	29	2	470	3	.617	58	462	4
Air Force	5	5	17	-12	0	27	16	1	334	4	.593	32	322	2
Utah	2	10	0	10	1	22	18	0	358	0	.818	24	368	0
San Diego St.	4	21	10	11	2	33	23	1	327	3	.697	37	338	1
*Penn State	8	29	11	18	2	59	42	2	576	2	.712	67	594	4
Totals: (Pass Efficiency: 175.5)	85	235	362	-127	6	412	265	15	4,560	32	.643	497	4,433	37

*Bowl statistics are not included in season or career totals.

COLLEGE RECORD GAME-BY-GAME (CONT.)

1990 Opponent	RUSHING					PASSING								
	Carries	Gain	Loss	Net	TD	Att.	Comp.	Int.	Yards	TD	%	Plays	TO	S
UTEP	4	6	9	-3	2	46	33	2	387	1	.717	50	384	1
Miami	11	32	25	7	0	54	38	1	406	3	.704	65	413	2
Washington St.	10	22	31	-9	0	50	32	2	448	5	.640	60	439	4
San Diego St.	3	0	30	-30	0	38	26	0	514	3	.684	41	484	1
Oregon	6	0	56	-56	0	57	33	5	442	2	.579	63	386	3
Colorado St.	3	8	5	3	1	38	26	3	316	4	.684	41	319	1
New Mexico	5	7	35	-28	0	41	26	2	464	5	.634	46	436	2
Air Force	2	7	1	6	0	43	30	0	397	3	.698	45	403	0
Wyoming	11	26	42	-16	0	50	35	2	484	2	.700	61	468	4
Utah	4	12	19	-7	0	50	28	2	451	5	.560	54	444	2
Utah St.	6	4	43	-39	0	50	32	5	560	5	.640	56	521	3
Hawaii	5	21	15	6	1	45	22	4	319	3	.489	53	325	3
*Texas A&M	4	18	45	-27	0	23	11	1	120	1	.478	27	93	2
Totals:	73	145	311	-166	4	562	361	28	5,188	41	.642	635	5,022	26
(Pass Efficiency: 155.9)														

1991 Opponent	RUSHING					PASSING								
	Carries	Gain	Loss	Net	TD	Att.	Comp.	Int.	Yards	TD	%	Plays	TO	S
Florida St.	6	18	28	-10	0	32	19	1	229	2	.594	38	219	3
UCLA	10	34	42	-8	0	46	29	2	377	2	.630	56	369	5
Penn St.	9	8	46	-38	0	26	8	1	158	1	.308	35	120	6
Air Force	8	61	19	42	0	30	20	1	340	2	.667	38	382	2
Utah St.	5	17	9	8	1	30	21	0	329	2	.700	35	337	1
UTEP	10	8	63	-55	0	39	22	2	378	3	.564	49	323	5
Hawaii	8	19	23	-4	0	20	14	0	225	3	.700	28	221	2
New Mexico	4	35	0	35	0	39	24	0	375	4	.615	43	410	0
Colorado St.	1	0	6	-6	0	28	23	0	337	3	.821	29	331	1
Wyoming	3	8	0	8	2	30	20	0	306	2	.667	33	314	0
San Diego St.	8	50	46	4	0	54	31	3	599	6	.574	62	603	4
Utah	3	14	20	-6	1	29	18	2	378	5	.621	32	372	2
*Iowa	8	12	37	-25	0	44	29	1	350	2	.659	52	325	4
Totals:	75	272	302	-30	4	403	249	12	4,031	35	.618	478	4,001	31
(Pass Efficiency: 168.5)														
Career totals:	265	739	1,105	-366	14	1,530	958	65	15,031	121	.626	1,795	14,692	
(Career pass efficiency: 162.7)														

*Bowl statistics are not included in season or career totals.